# PELICAN BOOKS

*Advisory Editors*: H. L. BEALES, Reader in Economic History, University of London; W. E. WILLIAMS, Director, the Army Bureau of Current Affairs; Secretary, the British Institute of Adult Education

---

## YOU AND MUSIC
### BY
### CHRISTIAN DARNTON

( A 68 )

A distinguished English composer introduces the ordinary music lover to the significance of a wide range of music old and new outside the traditional repertory of standard classics. No technical knowledge of music is needed apart from familiarity with the general principles of musical notation. The book includes a discussion of the nature of music, an explanation of the development of European music from its earliest effective beginnings about the eleventh century, and a brief history of the orchestra with descriptions of the instruments in use to-day. There is a historical graph-chart which shows the years when notable composers were born and died, and a list of over a hundred gramophone records carefully selected to display to the best advantage the musical heritage which is ours to-day.

*Howard Coster*

## THE AUTHOR

CHRISTIAN DARNTON was born in Yorkshire in 1905. He early evinced a passion for music, and commenced piano lessons at the age of four. His first compositions were written when he was nine years old. At fifteen he began to take lessons in composition, and studied under Harry Farjeon and Professor Charles Wood at Cambridge. In 1927 a concert of his chamber music was given at Grotrian Hall, London. During 1928–9 Darnton lived in Berlin, where he studied with Max Butting. Returning to England he took an appointment as music-master at Stowe School, and subsequently was Assistant Editor of *The Music Lover*.

Christian Darnton's compositions include concertos for piano, viola and harp; a considerable output of chamber music and several works for large orchestra. All of these works have been performed in Germany, South Africa, U.S.A., etc., as well as in England. His *Five Pieces for Orchestra* were among the three works chosen to represent this country at the Festival of the International Society for Contemporary Music which took place in Poland in 1939. His *Stalingrad Overture*, performed at the Royal Albert Hall in March 1943, was broadcast in December of the same year. Latterly he has taken a keen interest in music for the theatre, for films, and for amateur orchestras and choirs. The author is at present engaged on his third symphony.

PELICAN BOOKS

# YOU AND MUSIC

BY

## CHRISTIAN DARNTON

*Second (Revised) Edition*

PUBLISHED BY

### PENGUIN BOOKS

HARMONDSWORTH MIDDLESEX ENGLAND
245 FIFTH AVENUE NEW YORK U.S.A.

First Published in Pelican Books 1940
Second (Revised) Edition 1945

FOR

G. V. K.

MADE AND PRINTED IN GREAT BRITAIN FOR PENGUIN BOOKS LTD.
BY HAZELL, WATSON AND VINEY, LTD., LONDON AND AYLESBURY.

# SYNOPSIS

# PART II

# PREFACE TO THE SECOND (REVISED) EDITION

EVERY author is pleased when a second edition of his book is called for. In my own case I am particularly grateful to the publishers for their request to prepare a revised edition of this book. For not only does it afford me the opportunity to rectify some inaccuracies which were in the first edition, but it allows me to give the reader a necessary explanation concerning the writing of the original work.

I was engaged on the manuscript when war was declared in September 1939. It will be remembered that the Government of the day made everybody's flesh creep by envisaging immediate air-raids which would be on such a scale in London that every form of life would probably be extinct within a few days. The Government urged all those who were not compelled by circumstance to remain in the city to leave forthwith. Accordingly, I and my family packed up our household goods and departed for the country; where I continued writing about You and Music as well as I could.

It was not easy. All my books and music were in store. And when, some weeks later, I timidly ventured into London again, the British Museum (and all other museums) were shut. So I was marooned without any books of reference whatever.

This circumstance explains some of the errors which crept into the first edition. Other mistakes were due solely to my own ignorance, for which there is no excuse.

It was impracticable to issue the book with a warning note to the reader of these sad circumstances. I could but hope for the best. I am told, however, that several people have had orgies with blue pencils, and have indulged themselves with fierce attacks on me. However that may be (for only one of these adverse criticisms came my way), it seems that there has been sufficient demand for a book of this sort to justify a revised edition.

Re-reading the original book to-day is not unlike being confronted with some unpleasing photograph of myself, taken several years ago. I should have liked to have adjusted that vacant and puzzled expression, to have softened some of the glaring high-lights, to have modified the more obscure shadows.

I should have liked, had it been possible, to have recast the features entirely, in conformity with the changes that have overtaken me. Unfortunately, it has not been possible to do more than correct some of the more outrageous defects.

With this intention I have done my best to remedy matters, in the intervals of duty with the Civil Defence Service. Many sections of the book have been entirely rewritten, since, with the march of time, I have been brought to alter some of the opinions which I formerly held. Notably, I have abandoned to a considerable degree the very subjectivist attitude which conditioned my approach to many aspects of music. In addition, the sections on The Nature of Musical Thought, Occasions for Music, and some of the historical sections, have been expanded. So the reader will now get more (and, I hope, better) value for the war-time price of ninepence than he did before. Which is as it should be.

I should perhaps add that this book does not profess to be a compendium wherein everyone can find exciting details of his Six Favourite Composers. Indeed, many quite well-known composers have found no place in the following pages—not because they are in any sense unworthy, but for the prosaic reason that there is no room for everybody in a book of this size and scope. For example, there are more composers sinned against than Sinding, who at least had the distinction of having his piano concerto played by Busoni.

I should like to mention my indebtedness to many friends who have been kind enough to give me advice and assistance in connection with this present edition; principally Dr. E. H. Meyer, who has allowed me the privilege of reading in manuscript his book *The Epic of English Chamber Music*. The many stimulating suggestions he put forward with regard to the historical section in particular have been a most valuable contribution. At the same time, I must make it clear that responsibility for the book as a whole is entirely mine.

With this apologia I recommend you to get down to the business of reading the book, in the hope that it will be helpful to you—and music.

CHRISTIAN DARNTON.

LONDON, *October* 1944.

8

# PREFACE TO FIRST EDITION

THIS book is designed primarily for those who like music sufficiently to go to listen to it occasionally, for those who listen to music on the radio and on the gramophone. To write about music intelligibly and intelligently is difficult. To read about it is apt to be depressing. A certain number of technical terms are unavoidable; for this necessity I apologise. I have been compelled to assume that the reader knows where Middle C is on the piano and that he is conversant with the principles of musical notation by means of a system of lines and spaces on which various symbols are written. But it is not necessary for an understanding of this book that the reader is able to go to the piano and play music at sight.

Every time a composer is mentioned by name I have inserted in brackets the dates when he was born and when he died, when these are known. Most musical works cited as illustrations of my argument have against them an index number, thus: *L'Après-Midi d'un Faune* [24]. If the reader refers to the end of the book (page 146), he will find a list of these works in numerical order together with the composer's name and the index number of the gramophone record on which they may be heard. Wherever possible the reader should obtain access to the records so that he can hear the music for himself.

I should like to make special mention of my indebtedness to Mr. Cecil Forsyth's invaluable book, *Orchestration*, from which most of the details of the various instruments of the orchestra are freely drawn; to Mr. Edwin Evans for his kind permission to quote at length from an article, "The Great Schism," which appeared in *The Music Lover* when he was Editor of that paper; and to many friends, notably Mr. Edward Clark, who have been good enough to make suggestions, amplifications and corrections of the text.

CHRISTIAN DARNTON.

*I*

# THE PHYSICAL BASIS OF MUSIC

AT the outset of this book I want to be quite sure that the reader and I agree on what we are talking about. My main intention is to write as simply and clearly as possible about music. I can foresee that this aim in itself will be difficult, owing to the very nature of music, which is intangible. So I propose to start off with the bare bones of music. I cannot help it if they are very dry.

Let us try to arrive at a few definitions. This may be best done, perhaps, by first considering not what music is, but what it is not. Music, says Don Juan in *Man and Superman,* is the brandy of the damned. This may be so. But it is not like a picture or a statue that you sit and look at and take your time over contemplating. It is not even very like a story or a poem, in which you can stop and re-read a passage several times. In other words, it is not static. It is movement: movement of sound. This movement produces audible patterns. These patterns, discernible to the ear, are also visible to the trained eye in the written notes. They are of four kinds: rhythmical patterns and metrical patterns, much the same as the rhythms and metres of a poem; and the patterns resulting from the "line" of a melody and, ancillary to these, from the interplay of two or more melodic lines simultaneously.

Before we go any farther, two important distinctions must be made: the difference between rhythm and metre.

Rhythm, properly speaking, is the "swing" of a phrase. A phrase may be likened to a clause in written or spoken language. Two or more phrases (clauses) combine to make a Period (sentence). Both phrases and periods are bounded by Cadences, which are natural moments of repose, like punctuation.

Metre is the "pulse" or beat. It is very important to have this quite clear in your mind, otherwise confusion will result.

Nearly everybody misuses the word Rhythm. People ofte
talk of the " complicated rhythms " of dance-music. This
quite wrong. The rhythm of a ballroom dance tune is regula
to the point of monotony; and must be so, in the nature o
ballroom dancing, which demands regularly recurring two
or four-bar phrases. What happens inside those phrases i
often complicated in a more or less crude way. This is th
Accentuation. Strong accents are placed where the ea
would expect weak ones, thus making what is called Synco
pation.

To clinch the matter, and make sure of the distinction be
tween Rhythm and Metre, it is quite possible to alter th
metre without disturbing the rhythm. Thus:

*This is the house that Jack built.*

Here is the metrical scheme:

PHRASE

$$\mid \smile \smile \smile \mid - \smile \mid - \mid - \mid$$

Now let us alter the metre:

*This is the house that Jackson built.*

The metrical scheme now is:

$$\mid \smile \smile \smile \mid - \smile \mid - \smile \mid \mid$$

But the rhythm, the phrase, remains unaltered.

Again:

*This is the house that Jack Robinson built.*

Metre:

$$\mid \smile \smile \smile \mid \smile \smile \smile \mid \smile \smile \smile \mid \mid$$

The rhythm still remains the same.

Finally:

*This is the house that Nebuchadnezzar built.*

Metre:

$$\mid \smile \smile \smile \mid - \smile \mid \smile \smile \smile \smile \mid \smile \smile \smile \mid$$

It may be noticed in passing that in this last instance the
*sense,* the *meaning,* of the line is different. In the first three
instances the meaning is:

This is the *house* that Jack (Jackson, etc.) built.

But in this last example the meaning is changed by shifting the stress. So that we are now emphasising that it was Nebuchadnezzar (and not anybody else) who built the house. Thus:

This is the house that *Nebuchadnezzar* built.

Here, now, is an illustration of a simple rhythm with a literary instance from a nursery rhyme:

> I saw three ships come sailing by,
>     Sailing by, sailing by,
> I saw three ships come sailing by,
>     On New Year's day in the morning.

The rhythmical construction here is simple: two periods of four bars each.

$$
\begin{array}{cc}
\text{(1)} & \text{(2)} \\
\end{array}
$$

I | saw three ships come | sailing by,  
    (3)        (4)  
Sailing by, | sailing by,           } First period.

      (1)            (2)  
I | saw three ships come | sailing by,  
           (3)         (4)  
On | New Year's day in the | morning.  } Second period.

It will be noticed that in this instance each period commences on a weak beat. It is also important to realise that rhythmical phrases and periods are not necessarily, or even generally, bounded by bar-lines.

Now as to Accents. I have purposely chosen this instance, simple in itself, to demonstrate that the bar-line can often be a tyranny. The unknown composer of the tune to this rhyme was not subject to this trap. Its singers usually are. There is, moreover, no sort of excuse in any song for misinterpreting the rhythm, if the composer has understood his job properly: the words give the clue, as in this instance. The sense, therefore, is: " I saw three SHIPS come sailing by." Sung thus, the music makes sense. Only too often do we hear: " I SAW three ships come sailing by." Which is both grammatically and musically absurd.

As an example of such fatuity, one may examine the first line of the celebrated lyric from Tennyson's " Maud," as set to music by Balfe (1808–1870). That jaunty, Anglican cheer-

13

fulness makes it seem as if the young man was stressing that it should be Maud who should come into the garden. The whole point of his request, however, was that it was not the conservatory nor the dining-room, but the garden into which she should come. It is said that Tennyson was extremely annoyed with Balfe for this elementary blunder. For, as the song is written, it is impossible to make any other sense of it than the one dictated by that unfortunate tune.

To return to our Ships.

As I have just said, the composer of the tune evidently understood the poem. But it may be held by some that the bar-lines are misplaced. This is controversial ground. Discussions about the functions of the bar-line crop up like hardy annuals in most musical literature from time to time. In discussing the matter at all one immediately becomes involved in technicalities which are irrelevant to the purpose of this book. I propose to say no more than this: bar-lines are, in the main, a convenience for reading, like paragraphs or any other form of punctuation in literature.*

In this case, the first period begins with a weak accent— I *saw* three ships come—and has a strong accent in the middle —I *saw* three SHIPS come. This is the metrical scheme which, extended to its completion, is:

I saw three ships come sailing by,

Sailing by, sailing by,

I saw three ships come sailing by,

On New Year's day in the morning.

Having, as I hope, got this clear, let us recapitulate.

Music is movement. Rhythmical patterns form the basis of this movement. Inseparable from these are the Accents, which make the metrical scheme.

Arising from this definition of the elementary basis of music, we see that it is perfectly possible, by definition, to

---

* Bar-lines first became common during the sixteenth and seventeenth centuries, when they were freely used merely as an aid to the eye in the full scores of music which at that time had a rhythmical and metrical elasticity and flexibility unknown after the bar-line had developed into a tyranny which has tended to impose the rigidity of an unvarying recurring pulse. A revolt against this metrical monotony made itself effectively felt some thirty years ago.

have music which takes account of no other features than these two, Rhythm and Accent. In other words, beat out accented rhythms on a drum, and you already have music. True, it is music in its most primitive form. But no one who has heard oriental or African drumming will ever forget the pulsating thrill which really seems to have some elemental power capable of inducing a true state of exaltation.

Our next step is to introduce Melody; that is, an organised series of notes: to have, not only a drum of one pitch, or even of indefinite pitch, but to add a Tune. This may be sung or played on either a wind or stringed instrument.

In the simplest instance the Melody follows the accented rhythmical basis in unison. More highly developed music, however, soon breaks away from this simplicity; and the Melos, or tune, begins to have an independent life of its own. Men and women sing together. It is found that each sex has a natural division into high and low voices. The women are Soprano and Alto; the men, Tenor and Bass. All four voices sing the same tune at different pitches. This needs explaining more fully. And to do this I must digress.

*    *    *

Having got as far as mentioning Melody, which is an organised series of notes, we must examine more fully what we mean by this.

We are now dealing with different Notes. Every note is related to another by what is called an Interval. I am compelled at this point to assume that the reader knows where Middle C is on the piano. From Middle C play all the white notes ascending in succession: D, E, F, G, A, B, C. The Intervals from the starting-point are as follows:

Middle C to D = a second    Middle C to A = a sixth
  „   „ „ E = a third     „   „ „ B = a seventh
  „   „ „ F = a fourth    „   „ „ C = an octave
  „   „ „ G = a fifth

The phenomenon of the Octave is fundamental to the science of acoustics, or the study of sounds. Sound travels in "waves" in the air. These are caused by a regularly recurring series of vibrations of a wire or string, in the case of a piano or stringed instrument; or of a column of air in the case of a wind instrument. These vibrations set up sympathetic movements in our ears and result in the apprehension of what we call a Sound. The extreme musically effective sounds are represented by the lowest A on the piano (28 vibrations per second) and the highest C (8,192 v.p.s.). If ever you have the opportunity to tune down a string on a piano or other instrument you will find that the resultant notes become lower and lower in pitch until they become inaudible. The string is vibrating too slowly for our ears to apprehend. At the other end of the scale the common bat, while flying, emits so high a note that it is only when it lowers its voice now and again that we can hear a very high-pitched squeak. Its song, mercifully, is beyond our range of hearing.

In parenthesis a similar phenomenon occurs with light-waves, red light at the lower end of the octave having 400 million million vibrations per second and violet light twice as many.

Middle C is today pitched at 256 v.p.s.* This figure is more or less arbitrary. What I am leading up to in all this is the phenomenon of the Octave. The C one octave above Middle C has twice the number of vibrations per second: 512. C one octave above that has, again, 1,024 vibrations per second.

\* \* \*

We can now return to our Women and Men—Soprano, Alto, and Tenor, Bass—singing a tune. The differences between Soprano, Alto, Tenor and Bass are roughly a fourth or a fifth. Thus the ordinary soprano has a range of about Middle C to A, a thirteenth above; alto, from the G a fourth below Middle C to C a thirteenth above, and so on.

They all sing the same tune together at their various pitches. It is, in reality, only a single line of melody. Each moment of sound is said to form a Chord. A chord is defined as several notes sounding simultaneously. In the instance we are considering, of four voices singing the same

* Since this was written the question of standardisation of pitch has cropped up again. There is now a recommendation that the A above Middle C should be fixed at 440 v.p.s. In the eighteenth century there were three different pitches in common use. Of these the lowest, the *Tief Kammerton,* was approximately one-and-a-half tones lower than our standard pitch to-day. This may account for the impracticability of some of the music of the period when played at its apparent pitch. (See page 65.)

tune at different pitches, the chord remains the same throughout. We now have Harmony—a succession of chords. This style of writing is known as Early Organum [1].

A fresh emancipation takes us one step farther. Each one of the four voices begins to lead a separate life of its own (Later Organum [2]). After a certain point in the development of complexity, it can be said that every one of the four voices constitutes a separate melodic line. This is Counterpoint—the interplay of several independent melodic lines which yet fuse into an organic unity—which may be exemplified in the Sanctus from the *Missa Papae Marcelli* by Palestrina (1525–1594) [3].

With many apologies for this forbidding opening, I must touch briefly on a few more of the dry bones of Music before going on to something more lively.

We must take a look at the European Musical Vocabulary of Sounds. I have explained the phenomenon of the Octave, which is a misleading word inasmuch as it leads one to expect a whole divided into eight parts. So it is. But these eight parts are a selection only of the twelve equally spaced notes which comprise the Octave.* The ascending or descending series of twelve notes is called the Chromatic Scale (Greek *chroma,* colour). It must be clearly understood that it is only in very recent times indeed that the vocabulary of music has included all of these twelve notes. It has been the usual custom to select from these twelve notes seven, or even five only, which the composer has used as the sole basis of his musical thought. The reason for this is that the natural harmonic scale has been taken as what may be called the fundamental premise of music all over the world. (See page 41.) (But see also pages 102 *et seq.*)

* By " equally spaced notes " I mean that every note is divided from its neighbour by a mathematically equal interval. By dividing the octave Middle C (256 v.p.s.) and the C above it (512 v.p.s.) into twelve equal parts, it will be seen that the difference between every semitone, or adjacent note, is governed by a common factor, making a geometrical progression. This factor is $\sqrt[12]{2}$, or $1\cdot05946$. This is only theoretical perfection. Without going into the matter fully, it may be said that it is found that fractions of vibrations occur in this scheme. These are eliminated by raising some notes and lowering others. The difference between adjacent semitones then, in actual fact, works out at about 6 per cent. (For fuller explanation of this rather difficult subject see the section on the Genesis of Music, page 102. Consult also Jeans' *Science and Music.*

17

It must suffice to say that this or that series of notes, known as a Scale, or more properly a Mode, forms the basic vocabulary of music.

To give an example: the Pentatonic Scales (Five-note Scales) form the basis of all known music in cultures which have reached a certain level.

One of these Pentatonic Scales corresponds to the five black notes on the piano keyboard. It is a rather startling thought that out of some one or other of these five-note systems the great majority of the world's music has been built. They are found in all European folk-music, in Javanese [4], Bali [5] and Chinese [6] music. My knowledge does not extend beyond these limits. But I dare say that the five-note principle can be shown to extend farther.

Certainly there are plenty of familiar examples to hand. *Auld Lang Syne* and the recent popular song *I've got spurs that jingle, jangle, jingle* are two out of many tunes which are built entirely on five notes.

For the present, all I wish to say is that two fundamental things assert themselves in music all over the world: these are the fixed Tonic, or key-note, around which the melody can clearly be shown to revolve; and the Dominant, the note a fifth above the Tonic—where C is the Tonic, G is the Dominant. These two focal points may be regarded as the primary relationships, being simultaneously antithetic, sympathetic, contrasting and unifying.

The Indians, for example, may divide their octave into five, six or seven parts (as indeed they do). Nevertheless the relationship between the Tonic and Dominant is as marked as it is in ancient Jewish, Arab, Polynesian and European music.

Further mention of this subject is made in the section on Notation (page 39).

Before we dismiss in a few lines such a subject, which has already been treated in many books, I must finally explain the nature of what are called the Church Modes.

These, too, have been the subject of learned treatises. I do not intend to expatiate on these either. The limits of this book are bounded by practical application of the present-day listener to music in ordinary currency.

The ancient Christian Church employed various vocabularies, or Modes, which were in common use up to three hundred years ago. They correspond roughly to scales played on the white notes of the piano beginning on D, E, F, G, A, B, C in turn. These Modes have tiresome names with which I will not burden your memory. Of these Modes only two have come down to us. The remainder were outmoded. These two are the one starting on C and the one starting on A. These are now known as the Major and Minor modes respectively, from the facts that the C Major and A Minor Modes are characterised by a greater, or Major, Third and a lesser, or Minor, Third respectively—the Third above C being E (two whole tones) and the Third above A being C (one-and-a-half tones).

These Major and Minor Modes are of primary importance in all that follows. Bear them well in mind, as well as the fundamental relationship between the Tonic and Dominant. These points are of importance, inasmuch as what we are ordinarily accustomed to think of as "a tune" tends to start from and return to the Tonic, or Key-note; and any piece of music which has a subsidiary tune traditionally introduces this Second Subject in the key of the Dominant.

In the hope that we have got this clear, I now leave this for the moment. References will of necessity be made to these important points later.

\* \* \*

To recapitulate: These, then, are our primary definitions on which we must be agreed before going farther.

Music has as its basis a recurring series of accented rhythms. Wedded to this is an organised series of notes known as Melody. This combination, in its highest development, becomes Counterpoint: that is, the interplay of two or more interdependent melodic lines.

Music is the ordered succession of a series of sounds, this series consisting of an octave divided (in modern Europe and the Americas) into twelve equal parts.

(*A discussion on the function of silence in music, which, as far as I am aware, has escaped general attention, would take us rather deeper into technicalities than is desirable. But I should like to advance the view that silence should be recognised as more than a mere absence of sound. Silence is, in fact, indispensable in music; even if the periods of silence are so brief as not to be noticed consciously. Silence is the opposite of sound. These two opposites together form the unity which we call music.*)

## II

# THE NATURE OF MUSICAL THOUGHT

If at this point it is presumptuous of me to hope that you and I are agreed upon what we are talking about, at least I can surely say that by now you understand what it is that I propose to discuss.

We are not dealing with the plastic arts. We are not dealing with literature. We are dealing with music, the ordered succession of sounds, and what happens to them.

This, then, is the composer's world. He lives mostly in a world of sound-fantasy as opposed to the pictorial images of most people's imaginations and the word-images of the literary man. In practice there may not be such a sharp definition between the one fantasy-type and the other. There are quite possibly people whose day-dreams—whose fantasy-lives —do not include music at all. Possibly they never have "a tune running in their heads." I do not know. But I should imagine that most people are sometimes subject to this crudest form of sound-fantasy. All I am saying is that the composer is a type of person whose fantasy-life is spent almost entirely in sound-images. Beethoven (1770–1827), in a letter to a friend, wrote: "Every day I come nearer to the aim which I can feel, though I cannot describe it, and on which alone your Beethoven can exist. No more rest for him!" Again: "I live only in my music, and no sooner is one thing done than the next is begun." Such a person is, to say the least, musical. If, allied to this, there is what is commonly called a creative urge, he is a composer.

In the last resort, the composer writes music in response to the social urge to communicate ideas; ideas, moreover, which cannot be expressed adequately by any other means. It is this ineffable quality of music which constitutes one of the most formidable obstacles to any attempt to discuss its nature.

I know of nothing more difficult than trying to explain the nature of musical thought, and making it clear what kind of animal a composer is. There are several ways of looking at it. The desire to create is in all of us from infancy. Without going too far into the question, it is a matter of common observation that every child delights in *making* something. There is the man-god idea in all of us. At least, that is one way of putting it.

Another approach is the biological one. All life is a compromise, within varying degrees, between the organism adapting itself to its environment and adapting its environment to itself. The higher forms of life appear to spend most of their activities in the second way. Man's present environment is almost entirely of his own making. He shuts out the vagaries of climate by building houses and clothing himself. His feet are not swift enough: he rides animals, builds vehicles for them to draw, invents locomotives and automobiles. He refuses to be tied to the dry land: he builds boats, he flies. He has ideas: he must communicate them by the spoken, the written, the printed word. He transmits them through the telephone, by means of the radio. He feels the urge, caused by who knows what impulse, to please his eye in a different way from the mere contemplation of the life around him: he draws, paints. He even distils perfumes. He beats on a hollowed log, a drum. He blows down a reed pipe, draws a bow across a stretched string. He makes music.

In a sense, it can be said that a composer writes music because no other music pleases him adequately.

Since the composer is primarily, as I have said, a person whose fantasy-life consists mainly of sound-images, as opposed to the more usual visualiser, it follows that before we begin to take into account other factors in his make-up he must be an unusual person. Can we describe him more closely?

Lytton Strachey once said that it was probably always disastrous not to be a poet. It is an irritating remark. It has about it an air of pregnancy which proves on examination to be a purely fleeting inflation such as has deceived so many people who are at all apprehensive that there may, after all, be something in it. It has, further, the appeal of the slogan which, as aphoristic writers such as Shakespeare, Goethe and Shaw have realised, has the value of apparently putting in a nutshell that which can be properly expressed only in an entire book. It is, finally, a misleading statement. The implications are those which are contained in that other dictum that all men are liars.

In so far as either statement is true, it can be said that all men sometimes have poetic moments, moments when they transcend themselves and become almost-poets, like the drab

21

little man in James Joyce's story viewing the sunset across the Liffey; and all men often lie.

There is, then, some truth in Lytton Strachey's rather tiresome remark. What is a poet? A highly imaginative person, among other things. The quality of "imaginativeness" is common to all artists. That is, they retain in a marked degree the child's ability to create a world for themselves. In passing, it is one of the functions of art to create an other-world for those who by nature are able to appreciate what the artist has to say, as it were.

I must insist here that there is not and cannot be an absolute standard of beauty (or anything else) in these matters. I will return to this point in a moment. Let me first continue my portrait of an imaginative sound-fantast whom we call a composer.

I believe it to be the common experience of all creative artists that, on the completion of a work, they are filled with an elation, a sense of achievement co-existing with a passionate desire to communicate their latest work to sympathetic minds, a nexus of such feelings which may be comparable to those of a scientist on the solution of a problem in original research. All these, and possibly more, emotions and desires are intertwined so that now one seems predominant and now another.

Music, considered strictly as an art, is the youngest of the arts. Any art is a vehicle for the communication of ideas. Theoretically a musical idea should be expressible only in terms of sound; a pictorial idea only in terms of line, related planes and colour. And so on. Theoretically, I repeat, an idea expressed in one medium should not be capable of transposition into another. But this is not strictly true. There is such a thing as "programme music," music which, if not necessarily or always directly representational in an onomatopœic sense, nevertheless is attached to some literary label. This aspect of music will be discussed later.

Given the quality of mind—to use a clumsy phrase for lack of a better—capable of significant ideas, the rest of the work of composition is largely a matter of mechanics. We have now arrived at a point in our analysis when we can say that music consists of ideas and their treatment. By this I do not mean a necessarily deliberate act of routine construction: some of a composer's finest achievements can be arrived at in a flash of what is commonly called "inspiration "—a brilliance of the unconscious mind, if you like. On the other hand, an act of deliberate reflection, a consciously purposeful decision, can also be equally successful.

In short, the legend of the artist as a so-called romantic figure whose musical or pictorial thoughts obey no known laws and whose personal life must necessarily be interestingly outrageous is nonsense. Creative activity involves a great deal of real hard work, strenuous " slogging " mental labour which can leave the artist prostrate and exhausted.

Every one of us is compelled to believe that he is fundamentally " the right kind of person "—soldier, scientist, gentleman or thief. If we cease to hold this belief we commit suicide. Many of us—and this is particularly applicable to artists—are so convinced that we are of the elect, that we become active and even aggressive proselytisers. It may even be said that one of the functions of the artist is to proselytise and to proclaim: " Here is this work! It is mine! In it I reveal new beauties! Look and listen! "

Speaking for the moment as a composer, I must in a very real sense dissociate my music from what is consciously and controllably ME. I cannot help what I have done, what music I have written. It is no more me—and no less—than the shape of my nose.

Can I define the portrait more clearly still?

The desire for recognition and acclamation is present in all of us. It may well be said that in part, at least, the artist is an exhibitionist. It is surely true of what are called interpretative artists such as actors, conductors and musical performers generally. And why not? Since Freud came on the scene to enliven our bed-time reading a conventional stigma has attached itself to the term exhibitionist, as if any such manifestation were but the penumbra of some shadowy individual undressing at his window in the belief, usually mistaken, that the spectacle will interest the girl on the opposite side of the road.

As to the *nature* of musical ideas, the *kind* of music that a composer writes, I believe that it is beyond question conditioned by social environment. We all know what is meant by that loose term " eighteenth-century music." But why is it that Beethoven (for example) wrote music in the particular style (convention) that he did? Why didn't he write cantatas as Bach did? or waltzes like Weber's? Clearly, I think, Beethoven's musical ideas were conditioned by his social environment. The social unrest of his time, expressed in the French Revolution of 1791, followed by the wider consequences in other European countries, is clearly reflected in his music—as witness the *Eroica* Symphony (originally dedicated to Napoleon) and his opera *Fidelio*. The pietism of the early eighteenth century, itself a social symptom, is similarly clearly reflected in the chromaticism of Bach, the paid employee of the Church.* The glitter of the Congress of Vienna and the court of the Empress Marie Louise no less clearly produced Weber's waltzes.

The later phase of the " Romantic Movement " shows a distinct tendency of composers to rebel against the social (bourgeois-capitalist) society which they were compelled to serve for economic reasons. If, that is, the composer of this (or any other) period did not supply the kind of music for which people were willing to pay, he had to accept the alternative of " starving in a garret," there being no Public Assistance Boards in those days. And, in fact, this is precisely what happened in the period of the rising class-conflict to artists of integrity, who refused to prostitute themselves to the vulgar tastes of their rich *parvenu* patrons, and *turned in upon themselves* as the only means of maintaining their self-respect. Consequently, this introverted attitude produced an art that was rejecting the world and exalting the " individual " to an altogether disproportionate, and even morbid, degree.

Many people have lamented the apparent lack of any objective standard of assessment of works of art. This absence of criteria is most manifest in music and painting. One cannot discuss anything without attempting to translate it into words. One can criticise a book, using the author's own weapons. But how can one say anything useful about da Vinci's " Mona Lisa " without, for example, mentioning that elusive smile, the significance of which has puzzled many worthy people for four-and-a-half centuries? True, one can pick on technical conventions and observe the artist obeying or disregarding them. Even so, the poverty of real meaning in such " criticism " is shown in the fact that art-critics and music-critics borrow from each other's preserves and talk of " the rhythm of a line," " the orchestral colour " and so on. This is so manifestly futile a disguise of the impossibility of

* I must beg the reader to realise that this is a statement of fact and not a belittlement of Bach.

saying anything on these lines which has any meaning at all that the wise man reads no farther.

In short, it may be contended that, although a great work of art is always recognisable as such by some people, no definition of its intrinsic qualities is possible.

But this line of argument seems to lead us to the conclusion that any assessment of the value of a work of art is a purely subjective affair. In other words, that it is a matter solely of opinion. I believe that this is incorrect. The fallacy lies in the attempt to arrive at what learned people call the quiddity of an object: that is, the essential quality that makes it what it is.

I regard this point as of such great importance, since it affects not only our attitude to music and the arts generally but to the whole world around us, that I will try to explain as simply as I can precisely what is the issue.

A common object such as a stool is as devoid of meaning *in itself* as a tetrahedron, or any other shape. The meaning, the properties and functions of a stool can be understood only by reference to its *social purpose*.

In fact a stool would have no significance, it would not even exist, unless there were the need for someone to sit on it. The need to sit on an easily movable object which is more comfortable and more socially convenient than the ground could arise only at a certain level of culture. There are in the world to-day millions of people who ordinarily interpose nothing between the naked ground and the bare seat that God gave them. Yet, given the social opportunity, these same people are perfectly capable of acquiring university degrees of distinction. Any " race-theory " of " innate inferiority " is thereby refuted. The fact that they do not produce stools and pianos is entirely explicable by the formula : *the social conditions wherein such things can be produced, or are even necessary, are not present.*

A stool and a string quartet are expressions of a social necessity. *Their full significance can be appreciated only by reference to the social conditions which produced them.*

This line of inquiry, no matter what the subject or object may be, is the only one that can yield positive answers.

Similarly, an attempt to assess the value, significance or beauty of a work of art must take into account its *social function*.

The influence of the social environment on the composer

is, therefore, a determining factor in the kind of music he writes. And if one attempts to arrive at an analysis without taking the social factor into account, one ends only by formulating a sterile catalogue of unrelated subjective events. This is the source of the interminable wrangles over such questions as: " Is Beethoven a greater composer than Bach? "—which is pretty well on the same level as an argument about the relative merits of a violet and an onion. Few people, I imagine, would like their steak flavoured with violets; and fewer still would deliberately have a dash of onion on their handkerchiefs.

The section on the Genesis of Music will throw more light on this. For the present, then, that is all I propose to say about the materials of our subject.


## III

### KINDS OF MUSIC

BEFORE we go any farther I want to discuss briefly two supposedly different kinds of music. I will pose a question: Is music emotional or intellectual? More particularly, is there one kind of music that is emotional, another that is intellectual? If we say Yes, what do we mean?

First of all let us examine the questions. By emotional music we mean music that has its origin, as it were, in the heart rather than in the head, which latter we commonly suppose to be the source of that other kind of music which we wrongly, as I hope to show, call intellectual.

All thoughts, with the possible exception of calculations in abstract figures, that is, pure mathematics, either derive from the emotions or are strongly influenced by them.

It is, perhaps, too easy to read into the state of mind of a composer in the act of writing music many things that are not consciously or even unconsciously present. The opponents of the " bottled thought " school of composition, according to whom the composer sits and fills himself with lovely thoughts and then goes and writes a rhapsody, have a great deal to be said in their favour. Nevertheless, though it may be extravagant to suppose too close a connection to exist between a man's emotions and his artistic creations, that such a connection is there cannot be denied. This is more obvious with regard to literature than to music, which deals with abstract ideas. It is, for instance, easily demonstrable in the case of song-writing, where the music has a distinctive flavour taken from the text, or the composing of Programme Music, which purports to illustrate a definite story or programme. (I shall have more to say about this later.)

If taxed closer, I should say that to get much nearer to any definitive clue to the problem is impossible; since if the ideas in the composer's mind were reproducible in words he would write a book, not music.

I doubt very much the possibility of "intellectual" music. To think of music-writing in such terms is confusion of thought. I prefer to oppose the Aural aspect and the Visual aspect. Neither is separable from the other. In contrapuntal music, for example, the visual aspect plays a very important part indeed. And I am tempted to see a great significance in the choice of note-patterns on paper.

Returning to the question in this light, one must clearly differentiate between the state of mind of the composer and that of the listener. Obviously music cannot of itself be emotional, intellectual or anything else. In the same way, a steam-hammer has no effect unless it hits an object. We are up against something very like the potential energy of the physicists. And the measure of this depends on the object under the hammer. Therefore, when people say "modern music is ugly," all they mean is that its effect on them is unpleasant.

From this arise the stupid, unavailing and often harsh "criticisms," based necessarily on personal reactions. That same imagined piece of "modern music," cited above, is potentially capable of arousing every shade of feeling from bitterest distaste to ardent worship, the only approximate canon of exact criticism being the technical merits and defects in workmanship; and such judgment is by no means indisputable.

Just as no two people are physically alike, no two are mentally so: their psychological make-ups are different. Returning to our steam-hammer analogy once more: put two people in front of a machine that will give each a punch of thirty pounds, one will stagger, the other will fall down. The emotional punch of a piece of music likewise will have varying effects on different listeners.

Despite the vaunted Physiology of Criticism expounded by Mr. Ernest Newman, the thing, but for one factor, would resolve itself into an expression of personal reaction, the only things making criticism worth while being the writer's own musical qualifications for discerning faulty craftsmanship and whatever literary knack he may possess to make what he writes attractively readable.

I here deliberately emphasise by repetition that that one factor, which alone can rescue us from the intolerable conclusion that assessment of a work of art is purely a matter of opinion, is the ability of the critic (listener) to relate the particular work of art under discussion to some single feature which is a denominator common to all arts of all periods. I such a common denominator can be found, we shall be provided with a universal yard-stick which will enable us to assess the " value " of a work of art.

If there is such a common denominator, what is it?

All attempts to localise individual qualities such as " genius " and " artistic appreciation " have demonstrably failed to provide a solution to the problem. The answer, I believe, is to be looked for in the realms of some conditioning circumstance which acts upon all and sundry in varying degrees and in different ways. There is only one such conditioning circumstance to which we are all subject: and that is our *social environment*.

If, therefore, I may deal once more in one of those dangerous things, analogies, I would point to the old saw about the bad workman blaming his tool. If we do not like certain music, the fault, if fault it can be called, lies in ourselves. Mr. Newman, of whom I personally am a great admirer, is musician enough to see what there is to be seen in the music of Schönberg (*b.* 1874). But for him, as he frankly confesses, although all the machinery of music is there, the results when heard are not music to him, and mean nothing or very little to him. But that is a confession of a limitation in himself, not a criticism of the music. As far as I am aware, Mr. Newman is quite unable to explain why he does not care for such music. Any plea that Mr. Newman's eminence endows him with a peculiar sensibility is inadequate because, as it happens, his opinion on the subject of Schönberg is widely shared. If his opinion was shared by nobody,

28

ociety would very properly lock him up in an asylum, together with other unfortunates whose views on certain questions o one agrees with. We are compelled, therefore, to believe hat there is in the music itself some intrinsic characteristic vhich gives rise to so widely held an opinion. We will attempt o analyse this quality in the Section on the Genesis of Music.

All this has been a digression.

In conclusion, it may be said that there are not two kinds of music, the one emotional, the other intellectual, but nany shades of *intellectualised* music.

All thought, as I shall show in the next section, must be ast into recognised or recognisable forms to be communicble. This casting is a process of intellectualisation. The lifference between a Chopin prelude and a Bach fugue is undamentally one of degree; although it is true that at a ertain point the *amount* of intellectualisation produces a nusic that is distinctively different in kind.

Whether we prefer the minimum of intellectualisation, hat is, music that relies for its appeal on the emotion that gave it birth rather than on the more enduring kind that nas passed through the crucible of the intellect—which also, be it noted, can induce equally powerful emotional reactions —rests with ourselves.

## IV

## HOW MUSIC IS MADE

### (i) MUSICAL FORMS

In Section II I attempted to give an impression of the nature of musical thought. Having done my best to capture for the reader a specimen composer, let me try to show something of his musical activities before we put him in a killing-bottle and mount him on a pin as the first of the exhibits which, I hope, will presently come to light in the course of this book. It may not, indeed, be too much to hope that from time to time we shall be able to add to our portrait of him; for do not imagine that I am claiming that we have anything like enough data at present.

I now want to discuss the methods by which the composer communicates his musical ideas to the listening world. The first step is to consider Musical Form.

To make a musical idea, or any idea, communicable, it must be cast into a recognised or recognisable mould or form. A sequence of beautiful words may seem of intense significance to the person uttering them; may, even, give the listener a certain feeling of " atmosphere." But unless those words are arranged on some basis of conventional syntax and with some reference to an agreed grammar, the idea behind the words cannot be apprehended with any accuracy.

The questions of accuracy and truth are in this connection closely bound together. The degree of accuracy (truth) contained in a statement must vary with the nature of the thought, and therefore with the symbols employed.

The theoretical accuracy of a mathematical statement far exceeds its practical application: it is seldom that more than six places of decimals are of practical use, since, for the carrying out of an idea in, say, engineering, one-millionth of an inch is near enough to the " truth " of the matter —although physicists can deal on paper with quantities so small as to be beyond the limits of microscopic vision, these being bounded by the length of light-waves.

The vehicles of ordinary thought, vocalised sounds and their written symbols, are scarcely comparable in their ability accurately to convey " true meaning." The most that can be said is that words " work " for all ordinary purposes: and that is not saying very much. It is at best a loose statement, since much depends on the language employed.

Now musical ideas are essentially fantastic. The utmost care has to be taken by a composer to put across his ideas with maximum effect. Like other languages, musical language is constantly changing. From time to time new conventions arise, born of social necessity. Some persist for centuries; some drop out of use, perhaps to be resuscitated by a later generation; probably none is perpetual and immutable.

Basically comes the statement of the idea, generally the " tune " or motive. Just as most people can recognise a bad tune as bad, so some people can recognise a good tune badly stated.

It is, then, the composer's first care to see to it that by every technical resource at his disposal he comes as near as is physically possible to stating his basic idea accurately and comprehensibly. Its statement must be satisfying.

But depending on the nature of the idea is whether a

simple statement is adequate for the composer's purpose, or whether the idea and the musical implications latent in it should be, or are susceptible of being, expanded and developed. I should warn the reader that in saying this I am expressing a personal view—by no means an eccentric one. But one should, perhaps, take into account the dictum of that eminent French composer and teacher Vincent d'Indy (1851–1931) that any musical idea is capable of application as the subject-matter of a slight piano piece, of a String Quartet, or as the basis of a Symphony.

We had got as far as saying that the composer must state his idea, his subject, as lucidly as he can.

He must now " decide " what to do with his material. I say " decide " in inverted commas; since I find that in writing down the processes of composition it is practically impossible accurately to differentiate between a fully conscious and calculated act on the part of the composer and a semi-conscious or unconscious act which I have referred to as a brilliance of the unconscious mind (page 23).

In some cases, if he is lucky, the composer will have been asked to write a specific work. When that happens (speaking for myself) a train of thought is started in his brain. Again speaking for myself, once the request has been presented, the process of musical thought matures, for the most part unconsciously, even in sleep: it not infrequently has happened to me that either at the outset or during the composition of a work my brain has felt dried up. But on waking from sleep of a sudden it starts working. Underground, unknown and incalculable things have been at work to start or re-start the process. In such case, speaking of the initial conception of a work, in some mysterious way the material or subject-matter which either bursts suddenly or gradually emerges into consciousness is found to be suitable for the purpose in hand. Sometimes the material appears ready-made; sometimes it needs moulding, hammering and reshaping to the composer's satisfaction.

Just as you can frame an epigram, write a rhymed couplet, a quatrain, a sonnet, a double ballad royal, an essay, a treatise or a novel, so in music can you employ a variety of forms. Or you may invent one.

After a simple musical remark, corresponding to a statement of fact, comes what is known as Binary Form, which may be represented as A-B. This consists of an initial

31

statement (A) and a collateral statement (B), usually closely associated in idea-content. This Binary Form was frequently used in the various movements of a Suite, such as Bach (1685–1750) and Purcell (1658–1695) wrote. (See below: DANCE FORMS.) In these movements the second section (B) is generally founded on the inversion of A—that is, A turned upside down.

Next, we may take Ternary Form: A-B-A. This consists of an opening statement (A) in the " tonic key " (see page 41); a second, often contrasting, statement (B), generally in the " dominant key "; and a return to A, again in the tonic.

Mention should also be made of Rondo Form. The Short Rondo Form (*rondo* is Italian for " round ") may be cast in the sequence A-B-A-C-A. The Extended Rondo Form may be elaborated into some such scheme as A-B-A-C-A-B-A.

No musically inclined person should have much difficulty, after a little practice, in determining the form of any single-movement piece of music. The possibilities are limited in the nature of the case to achieve adequate presentation of the idea.

THE SONG.—No more than a brief mention of the Song will be made here. For the most part composers have allowed the form of the poem to condition the form of the music. Hugo Wolf (1860–1903) is generally cited as an example of perfect architectural construction [7]; though in my opinion the great French song-writers such as Gabriel Fauré (1845–1924) [8] and Debussy (1862–1918) [9] are in that respect his equals and musically his superiors. But in many cases composers have merely used the text as a peg to hang their musical ideas on.

DANCE FORMS.—There is one feature that is common to nearly all Dance Forms; and that is, that most dances are divided into first and second parts (usually of equal lengths) called Strains. The most familiar of the older dances is the Minuet [10]. But there are many more ancient ones, which survived up to a couple of hundred years ago, such as the Allemande [11] (or German Dance), the Pavan [12] (which seems to have been of Italian or Spanish origin, the name possibly deriving from the Latin *pavo*, peacock, from the spreading of the dancers' cloaks, unless, as some authorities state, it derived from Padua in Italy) and the Galliard [12] (a gay dance following the stately Pavan, of which Prætorius

(1571–1621), quoted in Grove's *Dictionary*, says, " it is an invention of the devil, full of shameful and obscene gestures and immodest movements "). All of these dances are constructed of multiples of four or eight divisions, these four- or eight-bar periods following the steps of the dances, just as do our modern ballroom dances of to-day. Some dances, however, which began as pure folk dances, were later appropriated by the ruling class of the day. The music became highly stylised until in many cases only the frame and peculiar structure survived to indicate that the Pavan, for example, or the Passacaglia was originally music to be danced to.

The Passacaglia [13] in particular is of interest in this connection. Of uncertain origin, it was purely a peasant dance. The name appears to be derived from the Spanish *paso*, a step, and *calle*, a street. It was probably a running dance. Its musical peculiarity lies in the fact that one tune persists throughout, being played first on one instrument and then on another, while the remaining instruments weave an embroidery around it. In later days this individual feature has been preserved, although the dance character has disappeared. The Passacaglia is the most difficult musical form to employ, and has attracted many composers, who find the unity of design imparted by the reiterated subject a fascinating vehicle for their ideas.

THE CANON.—Another example of a purely formal movement is the Canon, Round or Catch. This consists of a single tune sung or played by one voice, which is presently joined by a second voice singing or playing the same tune, maybe a fourth lower or a fifth higher. A third voice may then enter after the same number of bars' " start " has been allowed for the first; and so on up to any number of parts that the skill of the composer may contrive. The famous Canon known as *Sumer Is Icumen In* [14], supposed by some scholars to be the work of the monk John Fornsete (*d.* 1239), is a superb example.

THE FUGUE.—The full title of this type of movement is Fuga per Canonem—Fugue according to Rule. The Fugue is another purely contrapuntal structure, consisting of two or more strands of independent yet interdependent melodic lines. The most usual number of parts, or " voices," is four; but five-, six- and even eight-part fugues are not uncommon. To explain what a fugue is without using musical examples is rather like describing a spiral staircase without gestures or drawings. And one runs the additional risk of making it appear a cut-and-dried affair; which, in the hands of a musician of genius, it most certainly is not. However, let me see whether I can make myself understood, taking a simple four-part fugue as an illustration. The first "voice," not necessarily the top or treble, announces the Subject. Immediately the second voice enters with the same Subject (usually a fifth above or a fourth below), while the first voice continues with a subsidiary melodic line. The third and fourth voices then enter in turn similarly. This Exposition is then generally extended by the different voices, not necessarily in the original order of 1, 2, 3, 4, but perhaps 2, 1, 4, 3, reannouncing the Subject from time to time. Then there may be an Episode, perhaps based on a characteristic fragment of the Subject, leading to the Development, when the various voices chime in with the Subject, running through different keys, each entry following closer and closer upon the heels of the other in what is known as a Stretto, or drawing-together. Finally, in many orthodox fugues, comes the Organ Point. This is a long note (usually the Dominant) held in the bass, while the other parts play or sing the Subject in the closest possible Stretto. Often in this final Stretto the parts enter only one beat or one note behind each other. The climax is the close of the Fugue.

The Fugue just described is only one orthodox specimen of many possible varieties. But all simple fugues fall broadly into this general framework, with the frequent addition of a Counter-Subject, which is so contrived that it fits equally well when played above or below the Subject, and appears almost at every entry of the Subject, it not infrequently being itself developed episodically.

I append here a schematic outline of the three-part Fugue in E flat minor from the First Book of Bach's "Well-Tempered Clavichord" [15]. This is not to be taken as a detailed analysis. Its purpose is to demonstrate as clearly as I can the architectonic structure of a Fugue, so that the reader can see for himself the inherent symmetry of the form.

In this Fugue it will be noticed that a device common in contrapuntal writing is employed: the Subject is turned upside down, inverted, as we say, half-way through (indicated below by the word *inversus*) with a subsequent return to the original form (*rectus*). In addition, the Subject is played twice as slowly, the rest of the music continuing at the same speed

# Structural Outline of the Fugue in E♭ minor, Book I of the Well-Tempered Clavicord by Johann Sebastian Bach

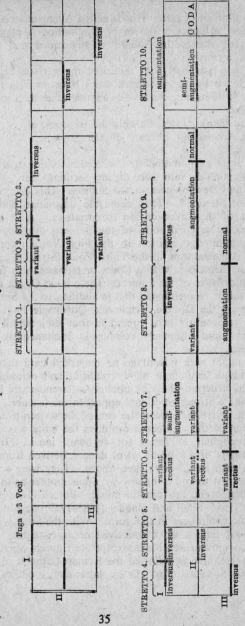

as before, of course. This is called Augmentation. In some fugues the opposite device of Diminution is employed. In complex fugues the Subject is augmented and diminished simultaneously.

I have purposely not indicated the various keys through which the Fugue modulates; for I have no wish to bring in complications unnecessary for anyone other than the technical student.

The blank spaces are episodic passages, all of them built on characteristic phrases of the Subject. There are ten Stretti.

A little examination of this schematisation will show that the Fugue falls into three distinct sections. First, the Exposition and Development of the Subject. This brings us to the end of Stretto 3. Then come the Exposition and Development of the Inversion up to Stretto 5. A return to the *rectus,* or original form of the Subject, introduces by way of a semi-augmentation in the First Voice (Stretto 7) the Full Augmentation in the Third Voice (Stretti 8 to 10). The Fugue then closes with a Coda, or tailpiece, also founded on characteristics of the Subject. There is no Organ Point.

It might be mentioned that in addition to the Simple Fugue there are the Double, Triple and Quadruple Fugues. These have respectively two, three, and four subjects, all developed in turn and ultimately combined simultaneously with one another.

It might with advantage be remarked here that although the Fugue is such a highly artificial and elaborate contrapuntal structure, the very qualities of architecture inherent in it make a strong emotional appeal to the listener.

THE SUITE.—Between the end of the sixteenth and the beginning of the eighteenth centuries the Suite was one of the most popular of forms for keyboard music. It consisted essentially of a suite or set of dances, derived from all countries, such as the ones cited above. They were so arranged in contrast to and sympathy with one another as to constitute the first cyclic art-form in music. Purcell (1658–1695) [16], Bach (1685–1750) and Händel (1685–1759) were notable and prolific composers in this form. With the Suite we have for the first time a work conceived of as consisting of several related movements, if we except the Church Masses, which, of course, always followed the Roman Catholic ritual.

THE SONATA.—For all its latter-day modifications, the

36

classical Sonata Form remains the most successful example of the achievement of unity of design on a large scale. The idea of the Sonata may be said to be latent in the Suite.

In this connection it may be mentioned that the word "sonata" means "something to be played," as opposed to "cantata," which is "something to be sung." Originally there were two kinds of sonata: the *sonata da camera* ("something to be played in a room"); and the *sonata da chiesa* ("something to be played in a church"). The *sonata da camera* developed into the Suite; the *sonata da chiesa* became the classical Sonata with which we are at present dealing.

Uncertain though the chronology of many of Bach's works is, it is probable, judging from the maturer style of his Sonatas, that they belong to a late period of his life. Bach's keyboard Sonatas are three-movement works: moderately quick, slow, very quick [17]. Haydn (1732–1809) developed the Sonata further [18]; his successor Mozart (1756–1791) further still [19]. The apex came with the Sonatas of the middle and later period of Beethoven (1770–1827) [20]. His piano Sonatas are mostly four-movement works: Allegro, Adagio, Minuet (trio), Finale (allegro or presto). The first movement of the Sonata is the idiosyncratic one associated with the term Sonata Form, or First-Movement Form. In essence this falls into four sections: Exposition, Development, Recapitulation and Coda. (*Coda* is the Italian for "tail.") Stated in full this becomes:

(i) Exposition:    (1) First section in tonic key.
                         (2) Transition, leading to
                         (3) Third section in contrasted key.
                         (4) Repetition of all, or part, of the
                                First section.

(ii) Development.

(iii) Recapitulation of (1), (2) and (3) in tonic key.

(iv) Coda.

The second movement is generally slow (in contrast to the general Allegro of the first movement) and may be cast in Ternary Form, Rondo Form, Theme and Variations, or even First-Movement Form.

In the case of a three-movement Sonata, the Finale is generally a Minuet or Scherzo (Italian for "joke"). This last is usually a Rondo.

Such are the general principles of Sonata construction. There can be many variations and elaborations. But I feel that this outline is sufficient to demonstrate the perfection of symmetry which was evolved in this form.

THE SYMPHONY [21].—The same form developed by Haydn is used for the Symphony, which is really no more than a Sonata for orchestra. But owing to the greater variety of "tone-colour" possible on an orchestra than on a keyboard instrument, Symphonies are generally considerably longer and altogether bigger works. It is true that such works lasting, maybe, for an hour, generally drive me out of the concert hall—so, you see, you are not alone. Nevertheless, it seems that there are some individuals hardy enough to withstand a protracted emotional onslaught such as this.

My objections are, firstly, that the emotion is not sustained: I have yet to hear a work of such length in which there are not dull pages; and secondly, that I am like a sponge, which can soak up only so much and no more. When saturation-point is reached, I can no longer listen, and fly incontinent out of hearing.

THE STRING QUARTET.—Once again Haydn, mentioned above in connection with the Sonata and the Symphony, is credited with the application of this same Sonata Form to the String Quartet, which before his day made only rare appearances more in the form of the Suite than anything else. Since this is not a text-book, I do not propose to go into the matter any further.

\*       \*       \*

We have now discussed the Physical Basis of Music. We have examined in some detail, albeit insufficiently as yet, the workings of the composer's brain. And in this present section I have tried to demonstrate the necessity for Musical Forms, and have put before you some specimens of such forms which are, or have been, in common use. It is understood that in all the foregoing I have made no attempt to be exhaustive. I cannot remind you too often that the intention of this book is to stimulate and arouse interest in the music you constantly hear, and thereby assist in a greater appreciation, that is, understanding, of all music.

We must now turn to the next step in composition: How does the composer write down his ideas?

We have examined the raw materials of music with which the composer works, and I have tried to give some picture of the artist and his mental processes. He has at his disposal twelve equally spaced notes to an octave. A piano has a range of seven-and-a-quarter octaves, this range extending to the utmost limits of musically effective tones. How, then, does a composer realise his intentions?

The first answer to this question is that, unfortunately for him, he very seldom does. He is not like the writer, who needs but pen and paper and a command of language for everyone in the world who takes the trouble to be able to read for themselves more or less what he means. Nor is the composer like the painter, who, though admittedly often misunderstood, has but to frame his picture, hang it on a wall, and induce people to come and look at it. Between the conception of a musical idea in the composer's brain and its realisation lie several steps, every one in itself unreliable and inadequate.

There is, firstly, the question of notation. The basis of our present system of indicating the exact intervals between the notes by means of a system of lines and spaces was laid down by Guido d'Arezzo (c. 990–c. 1050), who appears to have been a monk at the Benedictine monastery of St. Maur des Fosses. Prior to' his time various attempts at musical notation had been made, for the most part using letters of the alphabet or numerals, and subsequently a series of signs known as neumes (Greek néuma, νεῦμα, a nod or sign). But it would be out of place here to make an incursion into the realms of the specialist by even outlining the history of the development of notation. The interested reader is referred to the excellent article on Notation by Abdy Williams in *Grove's Dictionary of Music and Musicians* (Macmillan, 1920).

Musical notation as we know it to-day has been in existence for only four or five hundred years. And although several alternative systems have been devised since, the practical difficulties of changing over from established practice with the enormous bulk of printed music now in existence are alone a sufficient deterrent. Complicated though our present system is, it still has numerous deficiencies. There is no absolute standard of speed. A funeral march may be written in notes of identical " value," that is, of the same apparent time-duration, as a jig. It rests with the composer to supplement the written notes with verbal directions, such as Quick, Slow, Moderate—or their equivalent in some other language. Maelzel, who made an ear-trumpet for his friend Beethoven when he became deaf, invented an instrument called a metronome. This instrument has a graduated pendulum with a bob which can be moved up and down to vary the speed of the stroke. At each stroke it ticks like a clock. The composer may write music with three beats to a bar, and direct that the metronome is to be set so that there are to be 52 or 120 beats to the minute. But unfortunately music—apart from ballroom dance-music—is not so rigid; and the performer quickly finds that he is obviously outraging the composer's intentions if he attempts to keep strictly to this pulse. Apart from that, metronomes vary, so that the one the composer sets his tempo by may not tally at all with the one the performer uses.

Again, although the different shapes of written notes represent their relative duration in time, there is no provision for any time-values other than the second, third and fourth powers of two and, in a few instances, of multiples of three. Without expressly writing a little 5, 6 or 7, or what you will, under a group of notes, there is no means of dividing a beat into groups other than 2, 4, 8, 16 or 32.

To add to these difficulties, every "black note" on the piano has to be written in terms of one of its adjacent "white notes" raised or lowered half a degree, or semitone, by means of one of two symbols called sharps and flats respectively. This is particularly absurd. The reasons for this anomaly are as follows. In Europe the Octave is divided into twelve equal parts, or semitones. Hindu music divides the octave into 5, 6 or 7 parts, but varies the degree of pitch so that 60 or more divisions may be catalogued. The Japanese divide the octave into twelve semitones arrived at by tuning upwards in fifths. The Arabs make use of quarter-tones.* All these scales are artificial; but all of them are

---

* Alois Haba (b. 1893) has interested himself in quarter-, sixth- and even twelfth-tone music. These microtones, as they are called, fall on the unaccustomed ear with varying effects, depending on the sensitivity or tolerance of the individual listener. At an International Congress of Musicians held in London in 1938 I was one of those privileged to hear a demonstration of a specially tuned harmonium. This instrument was to all appearances normal. But its entire compass covered only the range of

40

based on the primary relationship between the fundamental note of the scale (called the Tonic), the Octave, and the fifth above the fundamental, or Dominant.

Scientifically speaking there is a true "natural scale" based on acoustic principles. This natural scale arises out of what is known as the Harmonic Series. Every note is accompanied by tones of higher pitch called Partials. They are not clearly audible on some instruments, such as the tuning-fork and the wide-stopped organ pipe. But the human voice and the piano, for example, are particularly rich in them. That is to say that a sound produced on either of these instruments does not consist of only a single note but of the Harmonic Series associated with it. When you strike, say, bottom G on the piano, you can, if the piano is perfectly in tune, presently hear its Harmonic Series as well.

Ex. 1

In practice you can seldom detect any partials above No. 8, the intensity of sound diminishing progressively. The bottom G is produced by the vibration of the whole string. The G above is produced by the vibrations of the two halves, the D above by the vibrations of the three thirds, etc.

If you use this fundamental G (for example) as the starting-point of your scale, the next note you can fix is the D which, when sounded, produces its complement of harmonics. From this series you can fix the fifth above D, which is A. Repeating the process, you can get a complete

a Perfect Fourth—from C to F above. When Dr. Sandberg, the inventor, played on this remarkable instrument, I for one found that the interval that produced the greatest sensation of physical pain was the Third of a Tone. It was curious to observe that no one in the audience was able to tell which of any two adjacent microtones was the higher in pitch. Interesting, therefore, as such experiments are—for what experiments are not interesting?—it is difficult to hold out any hope of a widespread popularity for such music. It seems likely to remain a scientific curiosity.

chromatic scale. Unfortunately, however, before you hav
gone very far, you will find that you have arrived at, say
E as the fifth above A, and will discover that this E is no
quite the same note as the E derived from C. The one wil
be slightly sharper in pitch than the other. Similarly with
the other notes of the scale: there are more than one versio
of each. Moreover, the intervals between adjacent notes ar
not equal. The untrained human voice always distinguishe
F sharp in, say, the scale of 'D major from G flat in the
scale of E flat minor, although on the piano the two notes ar
identical. String players tend to differentiate similarly.

In practice, therefore, each fifth is tuned slightly flat
otherwise the last note of the series, instead of being i
unison with the fundamental, would be slightly sharp.

The foregoing is necessarily technical and elaborate.
have tried to put the bare essentials as concisely as pos
sible. But the essential point to realise is that in the " natura
scale ", the octave is divided into *unequal parts*. Variou
methods of tuning have been tried in the distant past. Bu
it was not until the eighteenth century that Bach (1685–1750
popularised what is known as the Mean Temperament, in
which every note is a compromise so that the twelve division
of our octave are *equal*.

The first person to realise the full implication of this wa
Schönberg (*b*. 1874). As I shall show later in Section VII
where I trace the Genesis of Music, composers had during al
that intervening time been fumbling more or less blindly towards the important realisation that the " black notes " on the
piano are not in fact to be regarded as neighbours of the
" white notes " raised or lowered by means of a " sharp '
or " flat," as had formerly been the case, but were now separate notes in their own right, as it were. The octave is
now divided into twelve *equal* parts. Therefore there is no
reason why one note should take precedence over another
or be regarded as an " accidental," as notes qualified by
sharps and flats are called. In other words, the terms C
sharp and D flat, for example, should logically be abandoned,
and the note allowed a proper name of its own. If this
were done, one of the chief encumbrances of notation would
be cleared up.

Nevertheless, owing partly to the inertia of tradition, the
legend persists that there are sharps and flats—accidentals—
in our Mean Temperament scale.

These are the principal defects and deficiencies in our notation, and there is no overcoming them. Bearing in mind the extremely primitive methods of denoting relative time-values, as was mentioned above, and the entire absence of any standard of absolute time, it will be seen that the written notes are at best only an approximation to the composer's intentions, no matter how fully they are supplemented by verbal directions.

The next obstacle is the performer. He has to distil from these inadequate symbols what musical sense he can. The result, as everyone knows, varies sadly in direct relationship to the musical insight and general interpretative skill of the performer. When there are several performers, as in the case of chamber music and orchestras, the number of things that can go wrong in a performance is terrifying. The astonishing thing is not that the generality of performances is so bad, but that it is so good.

### (iii) THE INSTRUMENTS

Having, I hope, travelled with me thus far on the arduous exploration of musical territory, the next thing is to examine the instruments for which music is written. Up to now we have reached the point of putting it down on paper. But what are we writing for? There is a score of instruments to choose from. What are they?

There are four main kinds of instruments: wind (wood and brass), percussion, strings. These are subdivided into families:

Four wood-wind: flutes
oboes
clarinets
bassoons

Four brass: French horns
trumpets
trombones
tubas

Four strings: violins
violas
violoncellos
double-basses

The percussion we will leave for separate consideration.

I want to pause here to consider the incidence of these fourfold divisions. I remarked earlier on the four natural divisions of the human voice into soprano, alto, tenor, bass. It will be seen that the instruments of the orchestra follow this fourfold division very closely.

There is a further application of this principle which I may as well mention here, although it is not strictly in its place. I mean the facts that we have four fingers; that there are twelve divisions of the octave; eight notes in our major and minor modes. This is significant because, prior to Bach's time (1685–1750), it was customary to play keyboard instruments such as the organ with only the four fingers of each hand, the thumb not being used at all. Having regard to the other fourfold divisions mentioned above, when keyboard instruments such as the virginals and the organ were invented, the fact that men had only four fingers merely made the thing symmetrical.

Before we consider the instruments of the orchestra in detail, a history of the orchestra itself will not be out of place.

## (a) General History of the Orchestra

The orchestra as we know it to-day is a very recent development in the history of the youngest of the three arts, Music.

Surprisingly enough, the word "orchestra" comes from the Greek, meaning literally "a dancing-place." This referred to the arrangement of the Greek theatre in ancient days, when the dances were performed between the stage on which the dramatic representation took place and the space reserved for the chorus, in front of which sat the audience. Nobody seems to know exactly what Greek music of these times was really like, although several large books have been written about the subject. But these speculations need not concern us here.

We make a skip of many hundreds of years to A.D. 1600, when we hear for the first time something authentic about an orchestra that was anything more than a "consort" of instruments.

This was a little band of five instrumentalists, consisting of a viola-da-gamba—the precursor (not ancestor) of the modern

44

'cello, about both of which I shall have more to say later on —a harpsichord, a double guitar and two flutes. The occasion on which we hear of this " orchestra " was the performance in Rome of an Oratorio, *La Rappresentazione dell' Anima e del Corpo,* which may be translated as " The Representation of the Spirit and the Body," by Emilio Cavalieri.

Eight years later a landmark in musical history, familiar to all music students, was written: Monteverde's opera *Orfeo* [22], which had as orchestra two harpsichords, two violini piccoli—a kind of small violin now obsolete—two large guitars, two bass viols, ten tenor viols, one double harp, two organs of wood, two viole-da-gamba, four trombones, one regal—a small organ which survives only as a stop on the organs of to-day—two cornets, one little octave flute, one clarion and three trumpets with mutes. This all sounds very imposing. Thirty-five players! Why, modern chamber orchestras have no more.

Before 1650 the elements of the orchestra of to-day were established. There was a definite division into the four component parts of strings, wood-wind, brass and percussion. Such an orchestra was always written for by Purcell (1658-1695). Mozart (1736-1791) brought fresh innovations to be detailed later; Beethoven (1770-1827) still more, until we come to Berlioz (1834-1867) and finally Wagner (1835-1885), who both wrote for mammoth orchestras the like of which in size and complexity of the kind of music had never before been thought of.

Since then these achievements in sheer size have been surpassed, if we except the fantastic Berlioz, of whom the following anecdote is told. The King of Prussia, with whom Berlioz was having an audience, remarked, " I understand that you are the composer who writes for five hundred musicians." " Your Majesty has been misinformed," answered Berlioz. " I sometimes write for four hundred and fifty." And indeed he states in his book on orchestration that the ideal orchestra should consist of 242 strings, four of which are tuned an octave below the double-basses (!), 30 grand pianos, 30 harps and enormous numbers of wind and percussion players.

Such requirements are plainly impracticable; although when I was living in Berlin there was a performance of Mahler's (1860-1911) Eighth Symphony in which one thousand people took part. After all, the audience must sit somewhere, if they can bear it; besides which there is the delicate question of finance. Orchestral players are highly paid; and very properly, too. An ordinary symphony concert of to-day may, with two rehearsals, cost as much as three hundred guineas or more. If this seems a lot of money to some people, let them remember that good orchestral players are rare, and concerts rarer still, when it comes to making a living at the game.

Speaking of strictly contemporary times, the money question rules the hour absolutely. It is already a considerable undertaking to collect an orchestra of a hundred and twenty or so for Stravinsky's *Rite of Spring* [23], which is one of the largest scores of modern times. For whereas the dimensions of a Berlioz orchestra were due mainly to " doubling," that is, having more than one of a single kind of instrument, in Stravinsky's work it is actually the number of different kinds of instruments which make the orchestra necessarily large.

We see, then, that during its three hundred years of existence the orchestra has grown from a primitive group of half a dozen indifferent, even bad, players, to a perfect unity of organisation embodying from fifty to one hundred highly trained artists.

Let me go back a moment to insist again that there are few things in the history of music more striking than the enormous influence which the human voice has exercised over its every form. For the most part, when writing music for accompanying voices, which was nearly always the function of early orchestras, composers were content to let the instruments play in unison with the singers. It is therefore not too much to say that the nature and limitations of the human voice have actually conditioned the other forms of music down to within very recent times.

Additional limitations to the kind of music written for instruments were the imperfect methods of manufacture and the lack of skill of the performers. For some time, for example, organs were made with keys up to six inches wide. These were struck with the whole fist, one note to each hand. A slow business.*

* The organ cannot properly be regarded as an orchestral instrument. Yet I am unwilling to omit mention of it; if only because in the past its functions and influence have been considerable. Therefore, without embarking on a discussion of the

46

The earliest of the present-day instruments to attain perfection was the Trombone, in those days called the Sackbut (probably Old French *saquier-bucher,* to pull—to push), which was evolved from the trumpet in 1300 and has not altered its structure since the end of that century.

The second instrument to be perfected was the Violin, which achieved its zenith in Italy, where so many good things in music have come from, as early as three centuries ago, since when it has not been improved.

The latest instruments to be perfected are the French Horn and the Trumpet, both brass instruments, fitted with an arrangement of valves for producing their notes. It is the device of the valves which is the modern feature, introduced during the last century.

For some reason unknown to me, the backbone of the orchestra has always been the string section. The wind instruments as a rule have been used mainly to provide different tone colours in various combinations, but nearly always with the strings in the background. I see no reason

instrument itself, I will remark on the effects which it has had on, at any rate, two listeners. The following story is taken from a book with the charming title, *The Music of Nature; or, an Attempt to Prove that What is Pleasing and Passionate in the Art of Singing, Speaking and Performing upon Musical Instruments, is derived from the Sounds of The Animated World. With Curious and Interesting Illustrations,* by William Gardiner (1832):

" The writer, on Whitsunday, 1824, was in the organ-loft at Westminster Abbey, when the king and queen of Owhyee, Sandwich Isles, were introduced by the Dean, and placed near himself in the choir. The king, a vulgar-looking man, perfectly black, dressed in a black coat, white waistcoat, and pea-green gloves, which were not long enough to conceal his sooty wrists, stood up the whole time of the service gazing with amazement at the roof. The queen, a tall, fine masculine figure, was so struck upon the first burst of the organ, as to be thrown into extreme agitation, so much so, that she would have leaped out of the stall in which she was placed, had not her maid of honour (an English lady) prevented her by laying hands upon her. Every time the organ recommenced with its full volume of sound, this frenzy returned, and caused much confusion. During the sermon she settled down into something like composure, and at the conclusion was led out by the Dean and other dignitaries, to view the edifice. Habited in a fashionable morning dress, her majesty was only distinguishable from her attendants by her gaunt and gigantic figure, and the sudden ejaculations of surprise, which she was constantly making. The king, however, lost in mute attention, never lowered his eyes from the roof, but kept staggering about the church till he made his exit at the door."

why it has always been the tradition, and is still the rule, to have an orchestra consisting of, say, twenty-four violins divided into two " choirs," ten violas, eight violoncellos and six double-basses, while for the most part the wind instruments are represented singly or in pairs. It is a quality and balance of sound that somehow has become fixed in composers' minds. True, in Händel's day it was common enough to have as many as eight oboes all playing in unison. What it can have sounded like is inconceivable to modern ears. For the Oboe, of all instruments, is the most penetrating in tone. Suffice it that the convention of the predominance of the String Section has existed, and still exists, except for here and there a work like the Chamber Symphony of Schönberg (b. 1874) which is written for fifteen solo instruments.

And now a word as to the composition of the modern orchestra, which may be of three sizes: a full symphony orchestra, a small orchestra or a chamber orchestra. Beginning with the last, which is only the first pared down to its essentials, it is usual to have a small body of strings which preserve in themselves the tradition of the four natural divisions of the human voice into soprano, alto, tenor, bass, by having two sets of violins (" firsts " and " seconds "), violas and violoncellos, which last are usually reinforced by one or two double-basses playing an octave lower with them.

The number of strings in a chamber orchestra is always small: perhaps six first violins, four or five second violins, four violas, three or four 'cellos, one or two basses. In the wood-wind department it is customary to have one flute, one oboe, one clarinet, one bassoon; and in the brass, one French horn—two if you are lucky—one trumpet and one trombone, which last is invariably a tenor, trombones being made in two sizes, tenor and bass: a total of about thirty players. The essential feature of a chamber orchestra is that the instruments are treated as solo instruments; that is, as individuals; in contrast to the corporate unity of a large orchestra.

A small orchestra may have ten to twelve first violins, eight seconds, four violas, four 'cellos, and two or three basses; two flutes; one, possibly two, oboes; two clarinets; two bassoons; four French horns, two trumpets, three trombones (two tenors and a bass), with perhaps a Bass Tuba—the first mention we have made of this roaring giant of the orchestra, of which I shall have to reserve further mention until we treat of it separately. In addition, there may be a small " battery " of percussion instruments played by one or two artists—about fifty players in all.

Lastly, a full symphony orchestra, such as one gets at the B.B.C. Symphony Concerts, will have as many as thirty-six violins (twenty firsts, sixteen seconds); fourteen violas; twelve 'cellos; and ten basses; two or three flutes—which are made in three sizes: the ordinary flute, or *flauto grosso,* a tiny one, the *flauto piccolo,* and, rarely, a bass flute; two oboes; and a larger instrument of the same family called the English Horn or *cor anglais*; two ordinary clarinets, with perhaps a small one (E flat clarinet); one bass clarinet; two bassoons; one or two double bassoons; four, six or even eight French horns; two or three trumpets; three or four trombones; two tubas (a tenor and a bass); a full battery of percussion of various kinds, which may include three different drums as well as the kettle-drums or *timpani,* and cymbals, gongs, bells, etc.; one or two harps; and even a piano. That is, about a hundred players.

I cannot say who it was who set the pattern on which all orchestral scores are laid out. Certainly Bach arranged the instruments on his score just as we do to-day: that is, the orchestra is divided into its four families of wood-wind, brass, percussion and strings. Every score follows this arrangement, with the wood-wind at the top.* Furthermore, the detailed subdivision of the instruments is also stereotyped into four-part choirs, of which mention has been previously made.

I would like to insist for the last time on the fourfold division of all the groups of instruments on the vocal pattern. In the wood-wind the sopranos are represented by the flutes and oboes, the altos lumped together with the tenors being the English horn, clarinets and bassoons, the basses being also bassoons (these have a dual rôle) and double bassoons. In the brass, the trumpets are the sopranos; the horns, roughly speaking, the altos; the tenor trombones the tenors; and bass trombones and tubas the basses.

In conclusion, it will be seen that the composer must have a pretty extensive knowledge of all the elements which he has

---

* One exception is the MS. score of Schubert's *Unfinished Symphony,* which is in the National Bibliothek, Vienna. Here Schubert places the Violins at the top of the score.

49

to cope with. He must be able to hear "in his head" the exact tone quality of each instrument in all its registers—for the flute, for example, is weak on its four bottom notes (from Middle C upwards); the bassoon has a quite different quality in its top register from that in its bottom; the kind of trumpet in ordinary use in this country is agile and brilliant in its top notes, but poor and "slow to speak" below Middle C (its compass extends to the F sharp or E below); and so on. When orchestrating the composer has before him an almost limitless array of possibilities.

Naturally there exists a good deal of convention about "scoring," as orchestration is commonly called. I say naturally, because the composer is limited in his choice in so far as every instrument has its individual compass, or range, to the extremes of which it is generally for the player's sake inadvisable to go, and beyond which it is of course impossible. But in those many cases where the compasses of several instruments overlap, that is, round about the middle of the piano, the choice of mixing his colours is large.

But we seem to be getting into the realms of the specialist. We had better quit them immediately and go on to consider the orchestra in detail.

For convenience' sake, then, let us begin at the top of the score and work our way down, hoping to reach the bottom without stumbling too badly into the many pitfalls which beset the path of one who sets out to explain things to his fellows. For I am not omniscient, and can only try to set down what I know.

### (b) The Flute

This instrument cannot be traced in any form more than roughly resembling the modern Transverse Flute, to give it its full title, for more than four centuries. Antique flutes have been dug up in Egypt and Greece. But beyond the fact that they were wooden pipes with finger-holes there is no resemblance to the orchestral instrument of to-day, which owes its perfection to Theobald Boehm, who lived in the last century. Earlier types of flutes were blown in the manner of the penny whistle, whereas the contemporary instrument has a hole cut near one end as a mouthpiece and is held horizontally, whence its title of *Flauto traverso*.

There is no more confusing instrument in the orchestra than the flute. Certain of its bottom notes—its lowest is

Middle C, its highest, for practical purposes, the C three octaves above—resemble the quality of a trumpet so closely as to deceive even trained ears for a moment. Perhaps Debussy (1862–1918) knew more about the flute's possibilities than any other composer. His delicious *L'Aprés-Midi d'un Faune* [24] is a model of flute writing, exploiting its different qualities to perfection.

All of these points have to be borne in mind by the composer. He may, at a given moment, let the flute play a theme by itself. It may play in unison with the violins, or an octave above them. It may also be combined with any one, or several, of the other wind instruments. It may reinforce one of the horns. And each effect is different in sound.

Its conventional use is to give brilliance to the upper strings by playing with them, as long as the melodic line is smooth. Arpeggios, which are configurations based on blocks of notes (chords), although equally suited to it, give a quite different effect. Ravel (1875–1937) is very fond of this device, usually writing for two or three flutes running parallel with each other, such as, for example, beginning on the common chord of C major (C, E, G) and running up or down step by step. For an example of this style of writing the reader is referred to Ravel's *Daphnis and Chloe* [25].

There are also two other kinds of flute, as was mentioned above: the Piccolo (Italian meaning "small") and the Bass Flute.

The Piccolo, not so popular as its parent with poets, who love to rhyme it with Lute, is the most dangerous member of the orchestra. A modern writer has said that its lowest notes sound like a ghost with a pip in its throat. Throughout most of its register, however, its tone can be so piercing that the greatest discretion is needed in using it. At a moment of climax it adds an amazing brilliance to the score. Composers of a humorous turn of mind have occasionally made comic effects by writing duets for the Piccolo and Bassoon, the two instruments playing three or four octaves apart.

The Bass Flute is hardly ever met with. Only two examples come to mind. Appropriately enough the one is exemplary, the other a perfect specimen of what not to do. The latter is in *The Planets* [26], an orchestral suite by Gustav Holst (1874–1934). In this work the composer employs a mammoth orchestra of over a hundred, not counting a female choir, which makes a brief appearance for forty bars at the end of

51

the last movement—a monument of extravagance. The fourth flute plays also the Bass Flute. There is at least that economy, it being customary for the player to change from one instrument to the other where necessary—a simple business, the fingering and general technique being identical for all flutes. The folly of the Bass Flute in this instance is that, although used, it might just as well not be. It has exactly five bars of " solo work " right at the end of the last movement. In other places where it is used in this work one of the clarinets could just as well take its part and no material difference be apparent. Indeed, the composer has realised this, for he has written in the score a footnote to the effect that in the absence of a Bass Flute one of the clarinets can take its part. The other example, which shows off the beautiful, indeed unique, " sleepy " quality of the instrument is in the Action Rituel des Ancêtres section of *The Rite of Spring* [23] by Stravinsky (*b*. 1882). Here it introduces, and subsequently accompanies, a theme played in octaves on two muted Trumpets and a Bass Trumpet—another rarity. In this case, although the clarinet *could* play the Bass Flute part, the effect would be entirely different. Its use is justified.

## (c) The Oboe

We now come to the second instrument on the orchestral score—the Oboe; the most important solo melodic instrument in the orchestra, with a timbre that tends to be piercing, of biting reedy quality, capable of great sweetness in the hands of an expert player who, under the guidance of the conductor, must always be attentive to what is going on around him so that his tone shall blend as much as possible or shall stand out above the other instruments according to the demands of the moment. A single note misplaced by the composer can more easily upset the balance of the orchestra than almost any other instrument. It must therefore be used as well as played with the greatest discretion; and if only " single wood-wind "—that is, one of each—is used in a smallish orchestra, so that its use is unavoidable for the sake of " filling in," it must be so placed that, although it may not be intended to predominate, it will do the least harm if it does, as it will, stand out slightly more than the surrounding flute, clarinet and bassoon.

Its name may well be a puzzle to some people, pronounced, as it is in English, as if it had only two syllables, whereas the

Germans and Italians, using the same word, accord it three. We get a glimpse of sense in the word, however, when we turn to the French Hautbois, or old English Hautboy—" high wood," to distinguish it from the obsolete Gros Bois, " big wood." For it has the distinction of being one of the two surviving members of a large family which, in a rudimentary form, has existed since prehistoric times. In these early examples of the instrument's forbears the essential feature of a double reed is always preserved: that is, the mouthpiece of the instrument consists of two thin reeds bound together. These are inserted into the player's mouth and are set in vibration against each other, giving the instrument its distinctive tone. This is a distinguishing feature which it shares with the Bassoon, as opposed to the Clarinet, which has only a single beating reed, held against the tip of the pipe by ligatures.

The other survivor of the ancient family of Shalmeys, as they were called, is the English Horn, or Cor Anglais, which is no more than a distant cousin. But of this, more presently.*

The Oboe labours under the disadvantage of having the second smallest compass of any instrument now in use, the smallest being the English Horn. Its bottom note is the B flat below Middle C; its highest, the G two octaves above —a total range of two octaves and a sixth. It is also the most complicated of the wood-winds, having a formidable array of keys and finger-holes. Nevertheless, it is capable of great agility and " high-speed " work, which can sound very brilliant when properly employed.

A good example of its use is the opening of the third movement of Tchaikovsky's (1840–1893) Fourth Symphony [108].

Since Händel's day (1685–1759) the task of giving the tuning A to the orchestra has always devolved upon the Oboe. Everyone who has arrived on time at an English concert will have heard that long note given out, immediately picked up by everyone in the orchestra to adjust their pitch to. In more musically civilised countries such preliminaries are over before the audience begins to arrive. Useless, as is sometimes done, for the orchestra to tune up behind the scenes; the temperature of the hall will undo all the work

* For the sake of completeness there exists a Bass Oboe, but this is practically never used.

53

in the draughty artists' room. In his excellent "Handbook of Conducting," Hermann Scherchen, the great German conductor, says that it always ought to be insisted on that the orchestra are in their seats at least half an hour before the scheduled time of the concert, so that all the instruments are properly tuned and warmed up; for the temperature of the wind instruments makes a considerable difference to their pitch. That, alas, is an ideal unlikely to be achieved as long as orchestral players lead the hectic lives they usually do. It is no uncommon thing for an orchestra to rehearse for one concert in the morning, hurry off to a gramophone session in the afternoon at the other end of London, rush home to change into evening clothes afterwards, and arrive at the scene of the evening's operations as they swallow the last mouthful of a snatched sandwich, after which they are supposed to be in a calm and receptive state of mind to give a finished and artistic performance, as likely as not under a conductor whose acquaintance they made for the first time a couple of mornings previously at the first of the two rehearsals. That is why, until recently, when appraising a concert, one always inserted the proviso that in the circumstances the performance was as good as could have been expected.

To return to the Oboe: the instrument needs very little breath for producing its notes, a fact which calls for the finest control of the player's lungs, on which lengthy *legato* (smooth) passages impose considerable strain. Light chattering passages, on the other hand, are easy to play and effective. Innumerable examples of this kind of writing can be found in the opera *Hänsel and Gretel* [27] by Humperdinck (1854–1921), or in almost any work of Tchaikovsky (1840–1893).

We see, then, that although so severely limited in compass, the range of style suitable is wide: it can be tender or joking, sad or gay.

Despite the fact that its tone is so penetrating—not loud—at the first Händel Commemoration Concerts in this country twenty-six Oboes played in an orchestra against about forty violins. Since the Oboes of those days had heavier reeds than those employed now, in consequence of which the tone must have been even more piercing (and rougher), it is inconceivable what it can have sounded like.

## (d) The English Horn

The Oboe's distant cousin, alluded to above, is something of a poor relation. The English Horn, which is neither English nor a horn, is built on lines similar to the Oboe, except for two important points, and is the Alto voice of the four double-reed instruments, thus:

| | |
|---|---|
| Soprano | Oboe |
| Alto | English horn |
| Tenor | Bassoon |
| Bass | Double bassoon |

The differences in construction are these: the English Horn ends in a curious wooden "bell," not unlike a ball with two sections of the perimeter cut away opposite each other, one opening fitting on to the main pipe, the other free to emit air. At the other end of the instrument there is a thin metal tube on to which a double reed is fixed. This tube is bent, which gives rise to the theory that that instrument is not a *Cor Anglais*, but a *Cor Anglé*—bent horn. However this may be, it is in no sense a horn.

The bell at the end accounts for the unique tone quality of the English Horn. It has a deep hollow sound, quite different from the Oboe, more nasal in quality and more evocative of sadness. This virtue of the instrument has been admirably exploited by Berlioz (1803–1869) in the *Carnaval Romain* [41].

The instrument is pitched one-fifth below the Oboe—that is, its lowest note is the E below Middle C, its highest the A one octave above. This brings us to the first mention of what is called a transposing instrument. The fingering is identical with that of the Oboe. But, being pitched a fifth lower, as has just been said, if the player fingers a note which on the Oboe would sound G, the sound on the English Horn is the note a fifth below—C. This may sound confusing, but it is in reality the simplest from the player's point of view. And it is, after all, the player who matters. Imagine an oboist having to learn different fingering, which he would have to do were the notation "true to pitch," when his fingering is already the most complicated of all the instruments.

In a sense the Piccolo is also a transposing instrument. The fingering of the Piccolo is identical with that of the

Flute. But the resultant sounds are an octave higher. In this case it simplifies matters for the ordinary reader of a score as well as for the player. For if the Piccolo were written at its true pitch, the top line of the score would present the aspect of innumerable telegraph poles with all the ledger lines there would be.

The Bass Flute also is a transposing instrument, and for the same reasons. It sounds a fourth lower than it is written.

In the case of the English Horn the fact that the written notes are not the same as the actual sounds produced also in a measure simplifies matters from the point of view of notation: its most useful register lies between the treble and bass clefs. The device of transposition in the notation obviates the alternative of ledger lines or the constant changing of clef.

### (e) The Clarinets

The Clarinet differs in several important essentials from the Oboe family. First, it consists of a cylindrical tube of wood, whereas the Oboe and Bassoon family are conical in section; second, it has a single beating reed which lies against the tip of the tube, called the table, while, as described above, the Oboe has a double reed.

The Clarinet proper is a youthful member of the orchestra, dating from about 1690; although it was not in general use in the orchestra until a hundred years later. Since its introduction various amendments and improvements have been effected in the mechanism, which to-day consists of thirteen keys and twenty side holes.

Like the English Horn, it is a transposing instrument. It is, however, built in various keys: that is, it is of four sizes, the fundamental notes of each depending on the length of the tube.

The two in most frequent use are the B flat and A Clarinets, the former sounding one whole tone lower than written, so that a piece in the key of C major has its Clarinet part written in D, with a key signature of two sharps; the latter sounding three semitones lower than written, a piece in C major being written in the key of E flat.

In addition to these two instruments there are the Clarinetto Piccolo, the little clarinet, built in E flat, and the Bass Clarinet built in B flat. This last and the Double Bassoon are the true bass members of the wood-winds, the Bassoon being, as already said, properly a tenor instrument.

The Clarinet is the most useful member of the orchestra, in that its tone readily blends with any other instrument. In its upper register it can be shrill and strident; but throughout its compass it is capable of the softest *pianissimo* of very delicate quality. In addition, it is surprisingly agile. So agile, that in military bands Clarinets always play violin music in arrangements of orchestral music, which unhappily form the staple fare of that brilliant combination, so little understood in 'this country.

In consequence of the above qualities, it will be seen that the Clarinet has diverse functions. It can be a purely melodic instrument, or it can embroider the score with complicated arabesques, both in scales and arpeggios.

A good example of its use is Mozart's Clarinet Quintet [28].

It may be as well to mention that the Bass Clarinet is of such length that it is usual to find the bell of the instrument turned upwards, so that its lower part looks not unlike a Saxophone. I have seen a Bass Clarinet with a straight pipe; but apart from being unwieldy, it is unsatisfactory in that the player produces his notes into the carpet, which does not conduce to good tone.

The lowest and highest notes of the four sizes are as follows:

Ex. 2

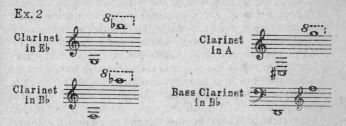

(The Saxophone is not generally regarded as an orchestral instrument; but one example of its use is in the popular Bolero [29] by Ravel (1875–1937). I therefore do not propose to treat of the Saxophones separately.)

### (f) The Bassoons

The Bassoon is the last member of the wood-wind family, about which not much remains to be said, since most of the things that are likely to be of interest to the general reader have been already touched on in the preceding sections.

If it appears that I am "drying up" it means only that what is applicable to one member of the group is in a general way applicable to all. And, indeed, I have already digressed from the instruments which I have discussed in previous sections to make passing reference to the Bassoon.

By the time we came to the Bass Clarinet the length of the instrument was already becoming a serious handicap to the player, as was shown. The Bassoon, being an instrument of eight-foot tone, would be quite unmanageable were it not so built as to bend back on itself in the form of a ∪, thus halving the length. Even so, an ordinary hand would have difficulty in covering some of the finger-holes were they not bored at an angle in the wood.

The early history of the Bassoon has been the victim of much confusion. In Italian it is called *Fagotto*, from its supposed resemblance to a bundle of faggots. This gave rise to the legend that it is a much older instrument than it really is, its invention being assigned to a certain cleric called Afranio, who is known to have built an instrument which he called Phagotus in the beginning of the sixteenth century. Eventually an old wood-cut of the good canon with his Phagotus was discovered, showing it to be something like a miniature organ blown by bellows.

Actually the development of the Bassoon has been a largely fortuitous business, successive makers improving by direct experiment upon earlier models. To this day it remains imperfect, many of the notes—which ones vary with the individual instrument—being indifferent in quality and shaky in intonation unless the player is skilful enough to correct the defects with his lips and by reinforcing with extra keys. Consequently the Bassoon player has to be on the watch as regards intonation in much the same way as a string player.

Many text-books advise the student to eschew the lowest notes as being poor in quality. I have never found this to be the case myself—and I used to play the Bassoon. Indeed, its bottom note, the B flat two octaves below Middle C, is peculiarly rich and full. Its top note, theoretically the F one octave above Middle C, has a curious tight, reedy quality. For practical purposes the top three semitones are ruled out. Whoever has heard Stravinsky's *The Rite of Spring* [23] will have noticed what nervous work the opening phrase is, beginning with a Bassoon solo on top C. It is seldom that this phrase "comes off" without a flaw.

The Bassoon shares with the Oboe the capacity for sardonic humour. It is always at home in staccato jumping passages such as Tchaikovsky loved. In its upper register it blends perfectly with the French Horn; in its lower, when played staccato, it goes very well with the Trombone.

The Double Bassoon is still generally regarded as an " extra " in most orchestras. This is a great pity; for the bass of the orchestra is its weakest part; and in default of a Double Bassoon the composer is often driven to scoring in the conventional and eventually monotonous way of having the 'Cellos and Double-basses in octaves throughout. This again is largely an economic difficulty. One way out of it is to make the Second Bassoon player alternate with the Double Bassoon. But this is at best a makeshift.

This concludes the wood-wind group. Next we shall attack the Brass.

### (g) The French Horn

The French Horn, known as the Horn for short, is an instrument of great beauty, most difficult to play well, and possessing triple functions; that is, it is used as a melodic instrument, for filling in harmonies as either a quiet or noisy background, and in later days has acquired some measure of pure decoration and embellishment. We shall, therefore, have a good deal to say about it. But before anything else, let us, as with the other instruments, consider its ancestors.

Primitive peoples have used horns made of conch shells, elephant's tusks and the like for signalling purposes. It has been, and still is, extensively used in hunting, especially in France, whence its popularity for this purpose gives it its name. It was probably introduced into the orchestra for the first time by Lully (1632-1687) as an instrument of brass winding round itself in a circle and carried, during the chase, over the shoulder. In 1711 we know from old records that it was used in the Theatre Royal at Dresden, and a little later was introduced into the Imperial Opera at Vienna. Campra, a composer now quite forgotten, wrote for it in his opera Achille et Déidamie in 1735; and Rameau (1683-1764) used two hunting horns in his operas. Their introduction aroused a good deal of opposition at first on the grounds of the coarse and noisy tone of the instrument. It is impossible nowadays to say how far these objections were justified; the instrument now in use is so far removed from its prototype that the sweet sounds we associate with it may well be as different from those of the old Horn as is the instrument itself.

The reader will remember that on page 41 of this book we referred to the acoustic phenomenon known as the Harmonic Series. It might be as well to turn once more to this page to refresh his memory with the salient facts of the Partials which are always found in association with the Fundamental Note.

It is on this phenomenon of the Harmonic Series that the Horn is based. Thus a simple Horn of about twelve feet in length is found to stand in the key of F. This means that the only notes which can be produced without artificial means—what these are will be gone into presently—will be the Harmonic Series beginning on the F one octave below Middle C, proceeding by successive steps thus:

Ex. 3

Harmonic Series

Horns of different lengths, thus standing in different keys, have similar series.

It was the player Hampl, at the Court of Dresden in 1770, who, to damp down the loud tone to which exception was taken, as mentioned above, stuffed some wool into the bell of his Horn, and discovered that the pitch was thereby lowered one semitone. He thereupon experimented by inserting his hand into the bell, and found that it was possible to produce notes other than those belonging to the Harmonic Series. True, the tone quality was different by being thus muffled. But this accidental discovery had far-reaching results. These stopped notes, as they were called, came into regular use in passages where the instrument was not too prominent.

Another invention was equally important. Music had long ago reached the point where departures from the opening key were usual. The drawback as far as the Horns were concerned was that none of the notes in the subsequent keys to which the piece modulated was playable on the instrument which had started so happily in the original key. It was obviously impracticable to carry about three or four separate instruments. The device known as the Crook therefore came into existence. This is a length of tube which is detachable from the main body of the instrument and can be replaced by another either longer or shorter, thus lengthening or shortening the instrument as a whole. This was one degree better. There still remained the serious disability of having to give the player time to change his crooks; and even then, of course, the notes he could play were limited in solo passages to the Harmonic Series, such as you used to hear Lord Lonsdale's postilion blowing on days when the Coaching Club met to drive down to Ranelagh; or the rather unsatisfactory stopped notes for less important passages.

During the last century a number of manufacturers busied themselves with perfecting a system of valves which by a simple mechanism cut off or open up different lengths of the whole tube. This done the instrument was equipped with a complete chromatic compass of notes, none of which needed to be stopped with the hand.

From the earliest times of the instrument's introduction into the orchestra it has been customary to have one or more pairs of them. This practice may be attributed in part to an attempt to reduce the limitations referred to above by having one Horn in F, a second in E flat, a third in B flat, a fourth in C. When they all stood in different keys it was naturally seldom that they played together. The custom of having two, four, six or even eight Horns in our orchestra has, however, persisted.

It is the invariable rule nowadays that the Horn in F is used, as being the easiest to handle. Exceptions are made when playing early music by, shall we say, Mozart (1756–1791), which of course was written for Horns in specific keys.

In one sense, then, modern scores are easier to read than older ones, in that the Horns are all in one key. For naturally the Horn is treated as a transposing instrument, for the same reasons as were mentioned above in connection with the English Horn and Clarinets. The Horn in F sounds a perfect fifth lower than its written notes, i.e. Middle C is written G above.

In earlier scores with four Horns, each pair standing in a different key, the chord of C major might have presented the improbable aspect of, say—

Ex. 4

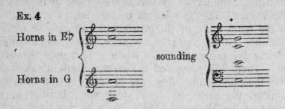

Horns in E♭

Horns in G

sounding

It is curious that the very obvious device of valves just alluded to did not come into being until so recently; for an ancient Roman Horn called the *Tibia* was discovered in 1876 at Pompeii. From its name those with a little rudimentary knowledge of anatomy will conjecture that the Roman *Tibia* was evolved from a shin-bone, which seems in some ways an odd thing to blow into. Anyway, this Roman Tibia had a system of valves consisting of eleven sliding sockets, any number of which could be closed at will. It has been remarked before that there is nothing new under the sun. However untrue that may be, it is disconcerting to find that such inventions are only rediscoveries, like the steam engine upon which the nineteenth century so prided itself, apparently oblivious that Hero had invented one at Alexandria in 100 B.C.

And now as to the functions of the Horn. Smallish orchestras always have two; large ones, four, six or eight, as already said. Whatever the number, they are written for as pairs, the first Horn of each pair taking the upper notes, the second Horn specialising in low notes. When playing softly the tone is sweet and pure, in some ways akin to the coolness of the Clarinet, but fuller and rounder. But it can also, as one writer has remarked, bark savagely like a wild animal or sound like a rout chair scraped over a parquet floor.

The classical instance of Horn writing is in *Till Eulenspiegel* [30] by Richard Strauss (*b.* 1864), where the Horn has the opening solo, beginning at the top of its compass and descending in wild swoops to the nethermost depths. Such passages must be written with caution, however. Strauss, being the son of a Horn player, knows as well as anyone what the instrument is capable of.

As a rule it is confined to smooth melodic passages and prolonged sustained notes. These last serve to cement the structure together when the rest of the orchestra may be executing more lively passages. In its more ferocious moments, such as the yells of the eight Horns in *The Rite of Spring* [23], that masterpiece of modern orchestration which I have quoted before and shall quote again, it can be really terrifying. It is a new aspect of the instrument which is in danger of being overdone, just as is the muted Trumpet, about which something will be said presently.

### (h) The Trumpet

One approaches the topic of the Trumpet with a certain diffidence. Not everyone calls it his favourite instrument. Shakespeare refers to "the harsh resounding trumpet's dreadful bray" in *Richard II*. And then there is that story about Mozart, which I do not myself believe, who is alleged to have fainted at the sound. On the other hand, I know a musician (not a trumpeter) whose favourite instrument it is. And Prætorius, writing in 1640, says "Der Trummet ist ein herrlich Instrument, wenn ein guter Meister, der es wohl und künstlich swingen, darüber kömmt." *

Historians for the most part seem not to differentiate clearly between the Horn and Trumpet families, adducing both from the common stock of early instruments made from animals' horns. However entangled its early history may be, we at least hear of the Trumpet when "Joshua rose early in the morning, and the priests took up the ark of the Lord. And seven priests bearing seven trumpets of rams' horns before the ark of the Lord went on continually, and blew with the trumpets; and the armed men went before them; but the rereward came after the ark of the Lord, the priests going on, and blowing with the trumpets. And the second day they compassed the city once, and returned into the camp: so they did six days. And it came to pass on the seventh day, that they rose early about the dawning of the day, and compassed the city after the same manner seven times: only on that day they compassed the city seven times. And it came to pass at the seventh time, when the priests

---

* "The trumpet is a beautiful instrument in the hands of a good player, who can manage it artistically."

63

blew with the trumpets, Joshua said unto the people, Shout; for the Lord hath given you the city. . . . So the people shouted when the priests blew with the trumpets: and it came to pass, when the people heard the sound of the trumpet, and the people shouted with a great shout, that the wall fell down flat." Joshua lived about 1200 B.C.

It is claimed that the instrument as known in China is of even greater antiquity. The clearest differentiation between the Horn and the Trumpet that we can make is this. The Trumpet belongs to the Tuba family, the parent also of the Trombone; whereas the Horn is descended from the Lituus. Both of these ancient instruments are met with in early Roman times—

> Multos castra juvant, et lituo tubae
> Permixtus sonitus.
>
> *Horace* (65–68 B.C.)

—and both are derived from other sources; the Tuba from the Etruscans, the Lituus from the Oscans.

It may be pointed out, in passing, that the modern Cornet is a hybrid descended from the two families. For the reason that the Cornet is regrettably absent from English Orchestras, no more will be said about it except that it is an instrument of four-foot tone, whereas the Trumpet is of eight-foot tone, which difference is accountable for its lesser brilliance. This is compensated for by its increased agility, which can rival that of the Clarinet. Its use in French orchestras is a recognised thing, and in Germany, too, it is frequently found. That we in this country do not employ it cannot be too much regretted.

The Trumpet suffered, naturally, from the same disabilities as the Horn, until it was furnished with valves in the last century, viz. it could play only the notes of the Harmonic Series. Like the Horns, too, the Trumpets were, and still are, built in different keys. The one in most frequent use in England is the B flat Trumpet with a compass from F sharp below Middle C to the B flat two octaves above. Usually, however, its part is written as if it stood in C—that is, as for a non-transposing instrument—the player transposing at sight one tone up.

There are still musicians who lament the disappearance of the F Trumpet, as having a greater volume of tone and an altogether sweeter quality. Players have, perhaps unfortunately, allowed the instrument to lapse into disuse on account of the greater difficulty of playing the higher notes as well as the inertia of production. It does not " speak " so easily.

There is also the Piccolo Trumpet, built in D, which can with ease attack high notes which are outside the range of the ordinary B flat instrument, as well as the rarely used Bass Trumpet.

It is still a matter of dispute as to how the players of Bach's time dealt with his Trumpet parts. He writes shakes and florid passages so high that in some cases even the finest orchestral players will not attempt them except on a specially designed instrument called the Bach Trumpet, of which only a small number are in existence. When occasion arises these instruments have to be hired or borrowed from the makers. Messrs. Hawkes, to my knowledge, have a very fine Bach Trumpet which can easily play these otherwise impossible figures. (But see footnote to page 16.)

It is unnecessary to describe what a Trumpet sounds like. Its misuse as a harmonic instrument, that is, one which can supply part of the subsidiary harmony in a passage where the principal melodic line is distributed elsewhere, is sometimes met with, but is to be deprecated. It is in such passages that the Cornet is needed. Usually, then, we find it used for heroic flourishes and the like. And in such passages a body of two or three Trumpets, such as is met with in the modern symphony orchestra, can sound very fine.

My last words in the section dealing with the Horn referred to the muted Trumpet, which a few years ago threatened to become the bane of the orchestra. Although, as Forsyth has said, the Trumpet suffers the mute more gladly than the other brass instruments, since it preserves its agility under this indignity, the Horn, on the other hand, perhaps owing to its larger bore and its greater difficulty of intonation, seems to resist partial suffocation.

It appears to have been the post-war (I refer to the war of 1914–1918) French composers who were mainly responsible for exploiting the muted Trumpet. The sound, in small doses, is fascinating. But, like everything else, an orchestral trick can rapidly degenerate into a cliché. When this is about to happen, I have noted that music proper veers away from it, and the cliché, whatever it may be, becomes part of the stock-in-trade of the dance bands, which in this case have enlarged on the matter and made of the once straightforward mute an instrument of torture which at the same time voices the wails of its victims. Moreover, the purveyors of dance-music do not stop at over-indulgence in the ordinary wooden or metal cone which is the usual Trumpet mute. More or less complicated sound-filters of aluminium are also used; and, as a final touch, players are frequently seen to blow their instruments into that symbol of man's indignity, the bowler hat.*

### (i) The Trombones

As I mentioned in the introductory section of the orchestra, the Trombone is the oldest perfected instrument in the orchestra. It has undergone no modifications of structure since the fourteenth century, when it was called the Sackbut. The oldest existing specimen is dated 1557, and was probably made by the famous player Hans Neuschel of Nürnberg.

In brief, the Trombone consists of a double length of metal tubing, two-thirds of which are taken up by the characteristic slide mechanism, the remaining third being the gradually expanding bell. The instrument is made in four sizes: alto, tenor, bass, double-bass. The first and last of these are very seldom met with, the first because its functions overlapped those of the Trumpet, the last because it has been superseded by the Tubas, of which more presently.

Since most composers have been largely ruled by convention, until recently it was almost the invariable rule to find a choir of three Trombones in an orchestra, it being laid down as a text-book maxim that a single Trombone by itself does not sound well; i.e. is not correct. Consequently in conventional orchestration the three Trombones—two tenors and one bass—move about in block formation of chords when they play at all. To escape from the tedium of

* It is claimed by Iain Lang in *Background of the Blues* (published by Workers' Music Association, 1943) that mutes were in fact invented by jazz musicians. This may be so. I complain here only of over-indulgence in their use alike in "straight" music as in jazz. I am in accord with Mr. Lang when he says that the introduction of such devices is justifiable if an effect is successfully achieved. It was perfectly proper for Erik Satie to introduce a battery of typewriters into the score of *Parade*. An American composer, whose name escapes me, even went so far as to write a work called *Aeroplane Sonata* for piano and bull-roarer. But these things should not be done too often.

'Cellos and Basses playing in octaves (the Basses being too weak to stand up to the rest of the orchestra by themselves), we find Stravinsky, particularly, using a single Trombone in their stead. Examples of this can be found in the *Violin Concerto* [31], *Symphony of Psalms* [32], etc.

Ordinarily speaking, the Trombones are the natural base of the Trumpets, since both belong to the same family. They are, moreover, unique among wind instruments in that the production of the notes depends upon an exceedingly accurate ear and a nice adjustment of the movement of the slide, which has no set positions any more than a stringed instrument has. The players of both Trombones and stringed instruments have to feel their way into the notes. Moreover, individual Trombones differ from each other, since inevitable variations in manufacture, as well as the fact that the sliding tube is necessarily larger than the stationary part, make considerable differences in themselves.

In some ways the Trombone presents many difficulties for the composer who is himself not a trombonist. One has only to hear works by composers who are, like Elgar (1857–1935) and Holst (1874–1934), trombonists to hear the difference

Ex. 5

between Trombone writing by one who really knows the instrument and one who merely knows about it. The difficulties are these: there are seven normal positions of the slide, producing the notes as shown in Ex. 5.

These seven notes are called the fundamentals. By varying the lip pressure a complete set of the Harmonic Series can be obtained over each of these fundamentals, thus giving a complete chromatic compass from B flat above Middle C down to the seventh fundamental E. Now, in order to write good Trombone music, the composer must have in his head a full knowledge of the position in which the player will have his slide at any moment. If he has not got this knowledge at his finger-tips, the player, although having in front of him a passage which to the ordinary musician looks easy enough, may be landed with the impossibility of moving rapidly from, say, the first position through the third, down to the seventh and 'back to the first. Bicycle-pump music, as orchestral players call it.

So much for the technique of playing. In timbre the instrument has a wide range, from a smooth and impressive *forte* to heroic bombast (beloved of Elgar) on the one hand, to staccato " pops " which, as mentioned in the section on the Bassoon, blend very well with that instrument. Its functions in the orchestra are rather hard to define. Perhaps it is the simplest to fall back on the conventional situation of the choir of three Trombones forming an independent unit in themselves, the first tenor being melodic, the other two supplying the necessary background. A case in point which comes to my mind is the Statue Music in Mozart's *Don Giovanni* [33]. Another instance is that Chorale-like moment in the Andante section of Brahms's Second Symphony [34]. An example of its use as a purely melodic instrument is in Ravel's *Bolero* [29], where the first tenor Trombone has a long solo passage, following, if I remember rightly, the Saxophone solo.

I should like to mention, in passing, the debt which music owes to the demands made upon both trumpeters and trombonists by up-to-date jazz. Many of the feats of virtuosity executed by jazz players may smack of the music-hall stunt. Nevertheless, the remarkable agility which first-class players show, as well as their ability to produce notes at the top extreme of the instruments' compasses, has set a wholesomely high standard for the orchestral player.

### (j) The Tubas

Considerable confusion exists, even among professional musicians, as to the different members of the Tuba family. I will not confuse the reader with the several types of obsolete Tubas which preceded the two which are in ordinary use to-day. These two are the Euphonium, or Tenor Tuba built in B flat, and the Bombardon, or Bass Tuba built in F. Both are non-transposing instruments.

Both the Tubas resemble each other in appearance. They are formidable objects, capable of great belching roars, but also able to produce notes of a peculiar soft sweetness. They are of such length that they perforce wind round and

68

round in serpentine convolutions terminating in wide bells.
The compasses of the two instruments are given below:

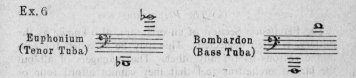

Ex. 6

Euphonium (Tenor Tuba)

Bombardon (Bass Tuba)

It is difficult to adduce instances of really effective use of
the Tubas, because they are so often grossly misused. There
again composers would do well to listen to military bands.
The beautiful Euphonium solos and the crisp, almost *pizzicato*
notes of the Bombardon sound brilliantly.

As a rule one sees on an orchestral score the word " Tuba,"
without any indication as to whether the tenor or the bass is
intended, and the part itself is as often devoid of sensibility
of the instruments' virtues.

Wagner (1813–1883) writes well for the Bass Tuba in the
Overture to *Die Meistersinger* [35], with which everyone is
familiar. Strauss (*b*. 1864) has written a very full part for
the Tenor Tuba in the Sancho Panza Variation of *Don
Quixote* [36]. Stravinsky (*b*. 1882) has used the Bass Tuba
to characterise the Dancing Bear in *Petrushka* [37]; and again
a most effective part for the two instruments in octaves in
the Cortège du Sage in *The Rite of Spring* [23]. The instrument can be muted, but not very satisfactorily. In the bad
old days it was not uncommon for the player to borrow the
harp cover and stuff it into the maw of his instrument.

In part, I may say, the confusion between the kinds of
Tubas that exists in the minds of so many people is due to
the unsatisfactory state of affairs within the orchestra itself,
where Military Tubas are, or were until recently, frequently
used in lieu of the true orchestral ones. I will not go into
the question further, as it will only confuse the reader the
more. It is a question which has to be settled among
musicians themselves: which instruments they really are
going to play on, what they shall be called and which
notation they prefer (there being the so-called Wagner Tubas
which are treated as transposing instruments, though whether

any such are actually in use to-day outside the opera houses I am unable to say).

That concludes the Brass Section. Next we shall tackle that neglected unit, the Percussion.

### (k) The Percussion

The Percussion Section of an orchestra, also known as the Battery, is often neglected. This may be as much for economic reasons as for any other. The managers of all but the largest orchestras feel that they cannot afford four or five " extras " to look after the " kitchen furniture," to use orchestral players' parlance; in consequence of which one, or at most two, players are supposed to be able to change over from Cymbals and Triangles to Xylophones and Drums as occasion demands. Composers, very properly objecting to such rough-and-ready methods, prefer to limit themselves to circumstances and write down their percussion parts to a minimum, not infrequently leaving them out altogether.

The Battery consists of two kinds of instruments: those of definite pitch and those of indefinite pitch.

To the first belong the Timpani, vulgarly called Kettle-drums, Bells, Glockenspiel, Celesta, Xylophone, Dulcitone, and, some readers may be surprised to learn, the Harp and Piano—both of which are essentially percussive in their nature, and consequently find their place in the orchestral score among the rest of the family.

The percussive instruments without definite pitch are more numerous. They are the Side Drum, Bass Drum, Tenor Drum, Tabor, Tambourine, Triangle, Cymbals, Gong, Castanets, and such special instruments as the Rattle, Wind Machine and Anvil.

Despite economic objections, we should be thankful for at least two things: the timpanist and xylophonist are specialists, whereas their colleagues are as a rule expected to be Jacks-of-all-trades, with the inevitable consequence that they are only too often masters of none. Thus the Bass Drummer frequently has one of a pair of Cymbals tied to his Drum, which he beats with his right hand, while he clatters away at the attached Cymbal with his left, unable to effect any gradation of tone or to employ the various striking techniques upon which so much of the Cymbal's effectiveness depends. Worst of all, some fiend has invented a cymbal-playing gadget which is operated by the foot. The resultant noise is such that the player might just as well be banging together a couple of old tin plates. The Italian name for Cymbals, by the way, is *Piatti* (plates).

Detailed consideration of these various instruments follows.

Timpani—frequently misspelt Tympani: there is no *y* in the Italian alphabet—are made in three sizes with a combined range of one octave—from F below Middle C down to the F one octave below. The resonating part of the instrument consists of a copper bowl, across which is stretched a parchment, forming the drum-head. By an arrangement of screws, or taps, the tension of this parchment can be altered. Consequently each of the Timpani can be tuned perfectly within the compass of roughly a fourth. The drum-sticks have flexible handles of wood, the heads being made of sponge, rubber or wood. Depending on the effect the composer intends, one or other of these sticks is used; though not many composers are careful enough to indicate their wishes in this matter. In this respect Berlioz (1803–1869) was a model. The score of his *Symphonie Fantastique* [38] bristles with directions to the timpanist to use first one kind of stick and then another. It is surprising to find that the Timpani came to us from the Arabs, who called them *Naqqareh,* a word which found its way into the English language in the form of *Naker* in the fourteenth century. Chaucer writes of them in *The Knight's Tale* (1386): "Pypes, trompes, nakers, and clariounes."

I have a strong feeling that Orchestral Bells ought not to have been invented. They consist of metal tubes of varying lengths slung on a frame. It is intended that they should reproduce the effect of church bells, which for mechanical reasons are never used in an orchestra: a bell which would sound Middle C would weigh over twenty tons. In practice Orchestral Bells are nearly always out of tune, and are seldom played well because there is often no specialist to do so. They should be hit right at the top of the tubes; otherwise the sound they give out is such a mixture of Partials that it is impossible to distinguish the intended pitch. Apart from this, the quality of tone is ugly and metallic in the extreme. The favourite ones in use are built in the scale of E flat, and have a compass of one octave from the E flat above Middle C upwards.

The Glockenspiel is an amusing little tinkly keyboard instrument—everyone knows Papageno's music in *The Magic Flute* [39]. There are two types in use in England, one with a compass from B flat two octaves above Middle C to C four octaves above; the other possesses an extra ten semitones below the bottom note of the first, bringing it down to the C above Middle C.

The Celesta is a small keyboard instrument of very recent date. It was invented in 1886 by a certain M. Auguste Mustel of Paris, since when many French composers of that day introduced it into their scores. Perhaps the best-known instance of its use is in the music to La Fée Dragée from the *Casse Noisette Suite* [40] by Tchaikovsky (1840–1893). The keys operate hammers which strike little metal bars. These are suspended over resonating boxes of wood. The total compass is four octaves from Middle C upwards. In tone it is of exceptional purity and penetration, and has the additional advantage that it cannot get out of tune.

The Xylophone will be familiar to all readers who have witnessed the remarkable agility of that otherwise somewhat cumbersome gentleman, Mr. Teddy Brown. The principle of this instrument is the reverse of the Celesta. It consists of wooden bars resting on tubular metal resonators. These bars are hit with spoon-shaped wooden strikers. The compass to-day is from the B flat above Middle C upwards for two octaves and a tone. The technique is rather like that of the Hungarian Cimbalom, which does not find a place of its own here as being so rarely used in concert orchestras. The Cimbalom has, however, been heard in London in performances of Stravinsky's *Renard*, which has an important solo part written for it.

The Dulcitone, or Typophone, mentioned here for the sake of completeness, is similar to the Celesta, in that it is a keyboard instrument. The sounds, however, are produced from a series of tuning-forks struck by hammers. I have never heard the instrument myself, and know of only one instance of its use: it appears in d'Indy's *Chant de la Cloche*.

We are now left with the Harp and the Piano. For these a very few words must suffice. If the reader's curiosity is not satisfied by the little I propose to devote to these, he must read up the subjects in one or other of the numerous histories of these instruments.

The Harp is a survival from the days of the Pharaoh of

the thirteenth century B.C. But of course the instrument in use to-day is profoundly modified—and improved in the way of size and mechanical action. Everyone is familiar with pictures of classical Greeks holding little harps in their laps. These instruments appear not to have had more than a couple of dozen strings. Nowadays, the modern orchestral harp has forty-seven. We first hear of the Harp in Western Europe in the twelfth century, when it appears in England and Scandinavia. Thence it passed to Ireland, where in course of time it became the national instrument. In Wales it soon developed into a chromatic instrument with three rows of strings. Forsyth says that Harps of this sort with nearly one hundred strings seem to have actually existed. But the elaboration of their manufacture and the awkwardness of their technique forbade their general employment even in Wales. Thereafter the instrument underwent many changes until, about a hundred and twenty years ago, Sebastian Erard, the famous Harp and Piano maker, introduced his Double-action Harp. In this form the instrument is tuned in C flat. Each string can be stretched or slackened by a pedal. That is, each of the seven strings of the octave; for one pedal operates all the C strings, another all the D strings, and so on. Each pedal has three positions, so that when all the pedals are in the top notch, the harp stands in C flat. When the pedals are moved to the middle notch, the instrument is tuned one semitone higher—C natural. And finally, when all the pedals are depressed, the tuning is in C sharp. The constant shifting of the pedals imposes a great strain on the gut of the strings and, I may add, on the guts of the player. The strings have to be tuned several times during the course of an evening, and not infrequently break with a loud twang—sometimes slapping the player painfully in the face—during a concert. Its technique is too complicated to be gone into here. Suffice it to mention one peculiarity: the little finger of the player is never used.

The modern Pianoforte has several ancestors in the forms of the Harpsichord, the Virginals and the Spinet. The main important difference between the pianoforte and all earlier keyboard instruments is that the wires of the pianoforte are hit with hammers, whereas the earlier instruments had plectrums with which the strings were plucked. Here again the history is very fully documented. Bartolomeo Cristofori (1665–1731), a Florentine Harpsichord maker, ranks as an important name in the history of the instrument. The English John Broadwood (1732–1812) is another. The first manufacturer to use an iron frame was M. Mangeot, father of the violinist, André Mangeot, who will be known to many readers as an active force in London music of our times.

With one word more we must be content. All the above instruments have this in common: their function in the orchestra is as a rule to be used as ends in themselves. This is an important point to grasp; for the other percussive instruments, which have no definite pitch, are in the main used only to underline a particular rhythm or theme in the orchestra. Only rarely do we meet with them as solo instruments.

We now come to those percussive instruments which have no definite pitch. Briefly as we dealt with the other section of the Battery, we can, indeed must, be even more curt with regard to the remaining section; for there is, in truth, not very much to be said.

The Drums can be divided into two families: those which consist of a single skin stretched across one end of a frame or vessel of wood, copper or earthenware; and those which have two skins, one drawn across each end of an open frame. To the first category belong the Timpani, of course. There are also the Tambourine and a hybrid monster which passes for a Bass Drum in the concert hall.

The Tambourine has come down to us through about two thousand years, remaining unchanged throughout this long history. Its single skin can be tightened or loosened by means of brass rods and nuts. The shallow frame is pierced at intervals to admit little brass plates, like miniature Cymbals, known as jingles, which are strung in pairs on wires. Properly speaking, the instrument should be confined to the theatre, for its very obtrusive noise becomes excessively wearisome. Apart from which it can be used only where some strong local colour, such as a " Spanish atmosphere," is needed; although one must admit that Berlioz (1803–1869) has made good use of it in *Carnaval Romain* [41].

The B.B.C. Symphony Orchestra uses the Bass Drum substitute referred to above. In tone it cannot really compare with the proper double-headed instrument, and the only reason I can imagine why it is used in its stead is that it is easier to transport. But I am not sufficiently informed in the matter to speak with authority.

The Side Drum, Tenor Drum and Tabor are all more or

less of a kind. The Side Drum has two or more pieces of gut stretched across one of the skins. These snares, as they are called, give the drum a peculiar rattling quality, which is very useful in a roll—one of its chief functions.

The Tenor Drum is midway in size between the Side Drum and the Bass Drum. Its shell, or frame, is made of ash wood and is cylindrical in shape. It has no snares. It gives out a peculiarly impressive and sombre tone in the concert hall, but cannot, as a rule, be heard to advantage out of doors, where it is most frequently heard, it being outbalanced by the general body of other instruments in the bands of infantry regiments, which all employ it.

The Tabor is not often heard outside the confines of Provence, where it is popularly supposed to have originated. There exists a Guild of Taborers, who are reputed to possess great skill in drumming intricate rhythms and metres. Bizet (1838–1875) has written for the instrument in *L'Arlésienne* [42].

There remain the Triangle, Cymbals, Gong and Castanets. The first of these was a favourite with composers of the last century to heighten an effect of piquancy or bizarrerie. But I doubt whether anyone would really call it his favourite instrument. Wagner understood its use as well as anyone: the Triangle part in *Die Meistersinger* [35] Overture is worth studying, though only for a moment, there being but one note.

"Cymbales be instruments of musick, and be smit together, and soundeth and ringeth," as a sixteenth-century writer, quoted by Forsyth, *op. cit.,* said. To be more precise, Cymbals are large brass plates, slightly concave, so that when hit together only the edges make contact. They depend for their effect on their size: the bigger the better, generally speaking. Elgar wants two pairs to be struck simultaneously in his Second Symphony, which argues that he was aware at the time of writing the work that most orchestras are badly equipped in this respect. A single Cymbal can also be hit with a felt drumstick with good effect; but the instrument should be treated with great respect if it is not to degenerate into that boom-clatter-boom which is still associated with the music-hall bass-drummer, who pounds away at his drum with one hand and batters the cymbals with the other.

The Gong is at its best when made in China. For some reason we in Europe seem unable to obtain the sonority of tone which the Chinese can produce out of a circular sheet of bronze turned over at the edges. Great care is needed in the striking of the instrument. It is all too easy to produce a dull bang instead of the *pianissimo* hollow boom or the galvanising crash which it should give out in *fortissimo*.

The Castanets were originally made of chestnut-wood (Spanish *castaña*), but are nowadays made of some other hard wood, hollowed out to give the characteristic "crack." In Spain these two pieces are known as *macho* (male), which is held in the left hand, while the smaller piece, *hembra* (female), is held in the right. My own surmise as to why the left hand should be regarded as male and the right as female, contrary to general European practice, where the sinister side of the family is the female line, is that in Spain the matriarchal tradition still lingers: it is no unusual thing to find a man bearing his mother's maiden name instead of his patronymic. This might account for the seeming prominence given to the *hembra* held in the right hand.

There are now only the rarely used freak instruments such as the Rattle, the Wind Machine and the Anvil. Strauss has written for the first two in *Till Eulenspiegel* [30] and in *Don Quixote* [36] respectively. The Rattle is of the old watchman's variety, with which the youth of this ebullient country is wont to enliven parliamentary electioneering meetings.

As to the Wind Machine, I can do no better than to quote Mr. Cecil Forsyth's entertaining description in his classic work, *Orchestration,* from which much of the above has been freely drawn: "The Wind Machine is not strictly a percussion instrument at all. On the other hand, it is certainly not a wind instrument except in the facetious sense. The sound-producing mechanism is a sort of barrel from which most of the staves are missing. In their place there is a covering of black silk. The barrel is laid on its side in a 'bearing' supported by an open 'cradle.' It is then churned round with a handle, so that the silk comes into contact with a 'face' of wood or cardboard. The instrument is used by Strauss in the Episode of the Windmills. The player is wisely directed to keep out of sight of the audience. This imitation of the 'felon winds' that blow 'from off each beaked promontory' may be itself imitated (pianissimo) in the seclusion of the home by means of two fingers and an umbrella."

The most famous use of Anvils is in *Das Rheingold* [43], where Wagner (1813–1883) wants to represent the toilers in the underworld forges. There was, as a matter of fact, a real Anvil at Queen's Hall. But as a rule a substitute is found in a set of small steel bars, which reproduce the sound well enough to deceive most people except professional blacksmiths.

## (l) The Strings

To give even a brief résumé of what is known of the history of Stringed Instruments would demand space greater than we can permit ourselves in a book of this scope.\* We must be content with just a few words about the several sources from which the two families of stringed instruments in use in the orchestra are derived, without saying more of the Guitar, Mandolin and Banjo than this: they are all descended from the mediæval Lutes, which formed a large family in the sixteenth to seventeenth centuries. Some historians make a distinction between the Lute and Guitar families. Admittedly they are of very different construction. Nevertheless, the principle of a body of strings stretched over a hollow resonating box, the strings being plucked in the one case by the fingers, in the other by a plectrum, is common to both. One point, however, must be conceded: that the Lute is of Arabian origin (Arabic *al'aud,* the word Lute being derived through a mistaken notion that the "1" of the definite article *al* is part of the word *'aud.* Only the Portuguese retain the word in full in the form *Alaude*); whereas the word Guitar is cognate with the Greek *Kithara,* whence, I should like to add, the word Gittern, or Cittern, of Chaucer's day, and the Hungarian Zither, Indian Sitar, are also in my opinion derived. The Lute is now obsolete. The Guitar and Mandolin are used only in those countries where one may stand beneath a lady's window and serenade her without contracting pneumonia. And the Banjo is generally relegated to what in my childhood were known as nigger minstrels—though whether any still exist I cannot say.

So we may comfortably turn to the Bowed Instruments, which to-day are divided into two families, represented by the Violin and Viol families.

\* Furthermore, there is some conflict of opinion concerning the origins of many of the instruments here briefly discussed. No doubt further research will explain much that is at present obscure, and even contradictory, in the evidence available to-day.

The latter of these has only one surviving descendant, the Double-bass. The Viols, which until 1940 were still made and played by that picturesque recluse, the late Arnold Dolmetsch, at Haslemere, were the precursors (but, it must be stressed again, not the ancestors) of the Violins. They undeniably possess a charm of their own, but are definitely inferior from the points of view of tone and general technique of playing. They were made in three sizes: the Treble, or Descant, Viol; the Tenor, the Alto and the Bass Viol, or Viola-da-gamba (Italian *gamba,* leg). There were various intermediate forms before the Violin was arrived at three centuries ago; but we need not bother with them here.

Historically it would be better to consider the Double-bass next. But we will adhere to our plan of working down the score and leave it until the bottom stave where it belongs.

The Violin family has three members: the Violin itself, the Viola and the Violoncello. In practice, I may remind readers, the general plan of the four-part vocal divisions is preserved by having two bodies of Violins—the " firsts " and " seconds "—the Basses, as a rule, " doubling " the 'Cellos by playing with them an octave below. There are, however, occasions when this four-part arrangement is subdivided. Depending on the number of strings available, the Violins, Violas, 'Cellos and, more rarely, the Basses, may be split up so that each section plays two, three or any number of parts up to eight.

Those of us who are not actually violinists, but who have had the opportunity of handling a Violin, might well pause to consider how many pieces of wood go to make the instrument. Let us see. Holding it in our lap longitudinally, so that it faces in the direction held when it is being played, we have at the extreme left the Scroll and the Four Pegs, the Finger-board, the Neck, the two Shoulders, the Ribs of each side, the " Hips," the Belly, the Back, the Tailpiece, the Tailpin, the Bridge, and, inside, the Soundpost. Nineteen main pieces, you will say. You are wrong. There are about seventy separate pieces of wood in most instruments. Of these about sixty are built into the main body of the instrument, the remaining ten being fittings.

In the preliminary enough was said about the general functions of the String Section of the orchestra for us to dispense with further reference now. Nor is it my intention to give an account of violin-playing, even were I competent to do so. It will suffice to remark in a general way that sounds can be produced by several methods. Normally the bow, which achieved its ideal form since Bach's day, when it was possible to play on three strings simultaneously, is drawn across the string, thus setting it in vibration and producing the notes. These notes are of two main varieties, open and stopped. The open notes are those which are given out by the natural tunings of the strings—G, D, A, E. These open notes differ materially in quality from the stopped notes, which are produced by placing the finger firmly on the string. There are also those sounds known as Harmonics. These are of two kinds, natural and artificial. The first of these are produced by placing the finger lightly on a "node," which is a point which breaks the subsidiary vibrations of the string and produces an attenuated sound one octave above the written note. (See the remarks on Partials, page 41.) The artificial Harmonics are produced by stopping the string with one finger on a given note and lightly touching it with another finger at the interval of a fourth above. The resultant sound is two octaves above the lower of the stopped notes.

The quality of the sound varies greatly with the position of the bow on the strings. Normally the bow lies more or less midway between the bridge and the end of the finger-board. For pianissimo playing, however, the bow is shifted nearer to the finger-board, and for certain effects may be moved practically on to the bridge itself. This style is designated *sul ponticello,* on the bridge. The resultant sound is a mysterious scratching not unlike that of a mouse behind the wainscot in the dead of night. It is in the representation of such tense moments, when the lonely watcher by the fireside feels as unstrung as the fiddle is liable to become, that this effect is mostly employed.

In addition, one sometimes comes across the direction *col legno,* with the wood. This means that the player taps the strings with the wooden part of the bow. This is not popular among players who, in the words of Mr. Forsyth again (*op. cit.*), prefer to keep the varnish on their fiddlesticks and the hair on their strings—both in their proper places.

No further mention need be made here of the various bowing techniques, such as *détaché, martelé, sautillé, jété,* the slur and the *louré.* But we may note that chords of two, three and four notes can be played. Of these, only those with two notes on adjacent strings, i.e. double-stopping, can be played together. The rest must be broken, owing to the curve of the bridge, which makes the sounding of more than two adjacent strings simultaneously impossible.

There is also the method of plucking the strings with the finger (*pizzicato*), the sound of which will be sufficiently familiar to every reader without further description.

All that has been said above applies equally to the Viola and the 'Cello. It would be as well to remark concerning the former, however, that its cumbersome size, taken in conjunction with the other factors, makes it one of the least satisfactory instruments in the orchestra. I know that I shall have all the Viola players in the country at my heels if the above ever comes to their ears. But in tone it cannot compare with either the Violin or the 'Cello, nor can it approach them in dexterity. The answer to this is that one should not attempt to compare them. Quite so. But in that case, the Viola should be a beast apart, and should not be called upon to supply the middle voice of the quartet which ought not to differ from its neighbours in any respect other than of pitch. The Viola is really an alto instrument. What is needed to complete the quartet is a true tenor.

We have now arrived at the last stave of our orchestral score: the Double-bass. As I remarked just now, this instrument differs from the rest of the string quintet in that it more closely approximates to the ancestors of the Violin family, the Viols. Some authorities believe that it is younger than either the Violins or the Viols, since it embodies the characteristics of each. For whereas it has the sloping shoulders and the flat back of the old Viola-da-Gamba, it has the four corners, the *f* sound-holes and the belly of the Violin. Until a few years ago it was the common practice of players in this country to hold the bow in the way in which the Viol bows used to be held. It is difficult to explain without a diagram the difference between the two methods. I will content myself with drawing a simile between the over- and under-hand grips of a tennis racket, these corresponding to the Violin and Viol methods respectively. In Germany the Viol grip is still in use, which explains why most music published in that country has the strong beats, which are, of course, down-bows in fiddle music, marked as up-bows for the Basses. The player, it may be remarked, sits on a special seat, rather like a clerk's office stool, to facilitate quick movement up and down the long finger-board.

The instrument has four strings, tuned in fourths from contra E to G. Formerly it had only three. But this instrument was smaller than the present-day one; and although the tone was much finer, composers so felt the need of the bottom E string that the sacrifice of tone was made. For some time it was not uncommon to see half the Basses in an orchestra with three and half with four strings. One or two instruments in London orchestras have an extra length of string which can be brought into action by a simple mechanism. This enables the player to get four more semitones, so that his instrument stands an octave below the 'Cellos.

Many people, including myself, feel the need for a radical change in Double-basses. The necessity of having exactly the right number in an orchestra is more urgent than for any other instrument. If there are too few they cannot be heard; if there are too many the combined tone becomes woolly and useless. London is fortunate in possessing some very fine players. All of these are virtuoso players and can give support to the instrument as of some solo value. But in general practice the Double-bass must bear the stigma of a unique distinction: it is essentially an orchestral instrument which has to be used, except in chamber orchestras, in large numbers to achieve its effect.

## (m) The Conductor

And now for the first time we mention the Conductor, who is of paramount importance in the orchestra. Without him, the finest orchestra in the world is like an engine without a magneto, a piano without a pianist, a race-horse without a jockey. It is he who directs, controls, subdues and excites his forces. Upon him depends ultimately the quality of the performance.

The original function of a conductor was simply that of a time-beater. Indeed, in the beginning of the sixteenth century no more was necessary. Consequently the chief singer in a choir, or the harpsichordist in an orchestra, or, in concertos, the soloist himself, was expected to set the tempo and, in moments when he himself was not too fully occupied, to beat time with his hand in the air, or with a roll of paper or a stick. In this last instance it was common at operatic performances for the conductor to beat time on his desk, in which connection I may quote the following from *A Comparison between the French and Italian Musick and Operas* published in London in 1709: "Some years since the Master of the Musick in the Opera at Paris had an Elboe Chair and Desk plac'd on the Stage, where, with the Score in One Hand, and a Stick in the other, he beat Time on a Table put there for that purpose, so loud, that he made a greater noise than the whole Band, on purpose to be heard by the Performer. By degrees they remov'd this Abuse from the Stage to the Musick Room, where the Composer beats the Time in the same manner, and as loud as ever. The same was observ'd in London six or seven years ago, but since the Italian Masters are coming among us, and the Opera's have been introduced, they have put a stop to that ridiculous Custom, which was founded more upon an ill Habit than any Necessity there was for it, as doing more harm than good, for the Opera's are better Performed now without it than any piece of music was formerly; because the Eye was too much Distracted, being obliged to mind the beating of the Measure, and the Score at the same time; besides, it kept the Singer and the Player in too much Subjection, and Fear of errors, by which means they were depriv'd of the Liberty, so absolutely necessary to Musick, and which gives a Strength and Spirit to the Notes."

At Spohr's first appearance in this country, on April 10, 1820, he astonished musical London by using a baton when he conducted at a Philharmonic Concert.

Conductors not infrequently have cut entertaining figures in the world. Perhaps M. Jullien, born in 1812, was the most eccentric. He founded the Promenade Concerts at Covent Garden. He introduced the firing of muskets into his celebrated quadrille, *The Huguenots*. At times he would be shot out of a trap-door, baton in hand, giving the signal to the orchestra to attack at the same moment. He invariably conducted all works of Beethoven in white gloves and with a jewelled baton, handed to him on a silver salver. Having in these ways astonished the world, he lost his entire fortune, was locked up for debt in Paris and eventually committed suicide in a fit of insanity.

A great deal more might be written about the functions of the Conductor, functions which of late years have reached unprecedented complexities which call for ever more and finer qualities of musicianship. Hermann Scherchen, whom I have already mentioned as being in my opinion one of the best conductors of contemporary music of to-day, has set forth what those qualities must be in his *Handbook of Conducting*. I recommend everyone, whether he be professional musician or not, to read it.

As was mentioned above, the primitive function of a Conductor is that of a mere time-beater. With regard to a properly trained orchestra of to-day, however, this aspect of his activities is practically negligible. At most—and this is important—some clear indication of the first beat of a bar must be given. But for the rest a conductor's gestures tend to indicate the moulding of a phrase, the adjustment of relative tone between the different instruments so that a proper balance and ensemble is secured, to ensure accuracy of attack and induce variations of speed where necessary. It is, above all, important that the Conductor thoroughly knows his score by heart before a note is played. When studying a work he must be sure in his own mind of the resultant sound at any given moment. He must know, for example, that if a chord is scored in a certain manner, it may be necessary to see that one of the Horns plays a little more softly than the player, who has only his own part in front of him and has no idea of what his colleagues may be doing, might otherwise do.

Instances of the need for constant alertness, thorough knowledge of each instrument's capabilities, and sympathy with many schools and periods of music might be given. But if I have indicated the importance which attaches to the player on the orchestral instrument, as personified in the Conductor, I feel that that is all that is necessary.

# V

## OCCASIONS FOR MUSIC

### (i) CELEBRATION AND RITUAL

I WANT the reader to keep clearly before him the scheme of this book. After examining the Physical Basis of Music, we discussed the Nature of Musical Thought. We then briefly glanced at some different kinds of music, and then expatiated on How Music is Made. This took us into a discussion of the necessity for Musical Forms; then we talked of the Notation used to write down the ideas; and lastly we ran over the Instruments on which music is played. I now want to write something of *when* music is played: Occasions for Music, of which the first I shall treat of will be Celebration and Ritual.

I think it is clearly established that all the communities which mankind has set up for himself, including our own, have been governed to a large extent by ritual observances. Various phenomena which, as mankind has progressed towards his emancipation from the darkness of unreason, apprehensive terror of what he has called the supernatural, towards rationalism and a fearless attitude to the realities of his environment (both internal and external), have caused him to set up a string of magical and mystical observances which in the main were designed to ward off imagined evils, propitiate gods which he from time to time made in his own image, and concomitantly praise with thanksgiving those same gods for the successful outcome of his major undertakings. Chief among these rituals have been those associated with birth, circumcision, the giving in marriage, death, wars, harvests and the succession of the seasons. All over the world mankind seems to have undergone these similar phases. In places as far remote as Peru and East Africa, which have never, as far as is known, had the slightest physical contact with one another, almost identical rituals have been the practice. Tottering on its uneasy apex, this particular civilisation of ours is still pocketed with relics from earlier cultures. Our growing-pains are accompanied by anguished struggles to cast off the heritages of past times. Here and there, in this twentieth-century England, little groups of people can still be found " praying for rain," as they quaintly put it. In peace-time they pray for the continued health and well-being of their sovereign monarch; in war-time they pray for the death of their enemies. At all times they pray for their young as soon as they are born, for the fruitful union of marriages, for the future of the " souls " of their dead. They observe ritual anointings with oil and coronations of their high priests and kings. They march to war with ritual and celebrate peace with ritual.

And for all these occasions mankind needs Music.

There is in my mind no question but that music does in

fact put a kind of Dutch courage into people. Music, more than any other man-made thing, has a potency capable of inspiring frenzy and of soothing distress. Music: anodyne, stimulant, narcotic, enervator. Music for weddings, baptisms and funerals. (In Europe the recently imported magical rite of circumcision has been rationalised into a so-called scientific necessity under such names as hygienic prophylaxis, so that the sacrificial knife of the priest has given way to the scalpel of the surgeon with all the blind authority with which medicine's high calling is endowed. One thing only appears to be missing in the modern version of this ancient rite: music, with the corresponding loss of performing rights to composers.) Music for war marches, peace marches, social demonstrations. Music for propitiations of gods, celebrations of harvests, prayers for deliverance from danger, prayers for atonement of sins.

All of these social manifestations, these group activities, still play an important part in the life of the community. Celebration and Ritual are the primary functions of Music.

## (ii) CONTEMPLATION AND EMOTIONAL EXPERIENCE

It must be hypothetical to estimate at what level of culture mankind first began to apply music to his own more immediate ends, to make music to be enjoyed by himself as an end in itself without reference to celebration or ritual.

It might seem that the shepherd boy as personified by the legendary Daphnis of Greek antiquity played his reed pipes purely for the pleasure he derived from doing so. His music may originally have had the function of driving away evil spirits who would cause his flocks to stray, of "keeping up his spirits" as we say. We know from the story also that his music acted as a love-charm on Chloe. Further, one can still see in the remoter parts of Europe a shepherd leading his flocks as he plays his pipe, with the obvious intention that they should follow his music.

But one has only to consider music in Europe up to certainly the fifteenth century to see that Art-music was still mainly the prerogative of the Church, was still intended for celebration and ritual; while the Folk-music consisted of Songs and Dances which, it is quite clear, were either survivals of pagan rites or expressions of popular feeling about topical social circumstances. Such music was the accompaniment to some activity: harvesting or such-like. And look at the English Sea Shanties: all are functional.

People were not yet sitting down to listen to music as an emotional or contemplative experience.

The precursor of such an attitude to music was the bard or wandering minstrel, whose main business was to act as a courier, messenger and revolutionary leader among the peasants. Hence, in times of social stress, Acts of Parliament were passed outlawing "musicians, rogues and vagabonds." The words of the minstrel's songs frequently had hidden meanings, a necessity imposed for security reasons, and were sung in alliterative verse (before the spread of Arab civilisation from the Mediterranean brought with it the rhymed verse which has stayed with us ever since) to the accompaniment of music. In such heroic tales related by the bards music was very much the junior partner in the entertainment. No one could read, therefore poetry could not be read: it was, as it should be, sung.

The first period in which music-to-be-listened-to can be said to have established itself must be during the sixteenth century, when we first hear of Madrigals and Consorts of Viols—what we to-day should call a little String Orchestra.

There are, of course, earlier examples, such as *Sumer Is Icumen In* [14], which dates back to the beginning of the thirteenth century. This remarkably lovely song, already mentioned on page 33, seems without doubt to have been absolute pleasure-music. But instances such as this are rare in music of the period. Therefore, as I say, the most convenient starting-point seems to be the fifteenth century in Flanders.

Now what kind of music was this early music-to-be-listened-to?

First the Madrigals. The origin and meaning of the word Madrigal are still obscure. Some attribute it to the Italian *madre*, mother, hence a song to Our Lady; others think it derives from the Greek *mandra*, a sheep, whence the pastoral character of most madrigals; while a third school of thought derives it from the Spanish *madrugada*, dawn, a morning song. However that may be, it seems clear that the Madrigal is descended from the songs of the old Troubadours and Minnesingers, itinerant minstrels who wandered through

Europe in the Middle Ages. The Madrigals were part-songs, mostly pastoral in character, and usually of considerable contrapuntal complexity. The earliest records of such Madrigals go back to the end of the fifteenth century. Rare examples are to be found in the works of Obrecht (c. 1440–1505), Josquin des Prés (1445–1521), Johannes Tinctoris (1446–1511) and others. All of these Flemish composers were primarily composers of church music.

From Flanders the Madrigal travelled. Arcadelt (c. 1514– c. 1560), a Fleming, migrated to Italy. There he published his First Book of Madrigals in 1538. This book was so popular that it ran through sixteen editions in eighty years. Costanzo Festa (c. 1495–1545) was the first important Italian composer to write Madrigals. After him came the Gabrielis, father (1510–1586) and son (1557–1612); Palestrina (1525– 1594), whose output of secular music was negligible in quantity; Vecchi (c. 1551–1605); Marenzio (c. 1553–1599), who had a big influence in England; Vittoria (c. 1540–c. 1614), who went to live in Spain, and whose music was also mainly ecclesiastical; Cavalieri (1550–ante 1600), who has been mentioned before (see page 45); Croce (c. 1557–1609), principally known for his church music, although his Madrigals and Motets, which are likewise secular part-songs, are very fine; and Monteverde (1567–1643), also mentioned above in connection with opera (page 45).

From Italy the Madrigal went to Germany, where it flourished considerably. A name which cannot be omitted at this point is Prætorius (1571–1621), often called the father of German music. After him came the famous trio of Schein, Scheidt and Schütz, born within a year of one another—1585, 1586, 1587. These three were the musical grandfathers of the great Bach (1685–1750).

In France the great Paris School, after a history of four hundred years, petered out with Firmin Carron in the middle of the fifteenth century, after which there seems to have been a lull in musical activity of importance until Lully (1632–1687). True, the French had developed their own Chanson, which may have accounted in part for the fact that the Madrigal did not take root there. But France was racked with wars during the period we are discussing, and for a long while after. Culture seems to have been at a low ebb.

In England several Italian Madrigals were published during

the sixteenth century; and by the last decade the Madrigal had firmly established itself [44].

At the same time a parallel development had been going on in instrumental music. This was the rise of the Viol family, which was invented in the fifteenth century. Viol music was pure and absolute music. The English were pre-eminent masters in this, which was virtually a new art. Fayrfax (d. 1521), Tye (c. 1497–c. 1572), Tallis (c. 1520–1585), White (1530–1585), Byrd (1538–1623), Morley (1558–1603), Farnaby (c. 1560–c. 1600), Bull (c. 1562–1628), Dowland (1563–1626), Weelkes (c. 1570–1623) and many other great names adorn the history of the madrigalists and violists of this island [45].

At this point the reader would do well to look at the folding chart at the end of the book to get a bird's-eye view of European musical history.

It must be remembered that although we are now talking of the beginnings of pleasure-music there was still no such thing as a Concert. Music was still played either on some special occasion, or, as in this period, in the private houses of the nobility and gentry.

It is important to note that this period saw the rise of the new "middle class" of merchants—the burghers (bourgeoisie) who were "those who lived in towns" (burgs, such as Hamburg in Germany, Cherbourg in France, Edinburgh in Scotland). One of the symptoms of the class-antagonism between this new class and the "common people" was a series of restrictive measures against, and even active persecution of, the people's music. Musicians were outlawed as "rogues and vagabonds." The reason for this is to be found in the fact that in all periods of acute social oppression the oppressed classes have been compelled to band together secretly in defence of their poor "rights." Music, frequently in the form of songs whose words had hidden political meanings, has at all such times been the vehicle of expression used by the people.* This, then, is the source of much of the

---

* Examples from later historical times are the songs of the Levellers in Cromwell's day, the Chartists of the last century and the American Negro plantation songs and the "Blues" of our own times. (See the *Background of the Blues*, already cited on page 66, for a most stimulating account of the social context of this particular kind of Folk-music. In addition, the reader is strongly recommended to consult *The Singing Englishman*, by A. L. Lloyd, also published by The Workers' Music Association, as this book is in the press.)

Folk-music of Europe. The non-functional Art-music has, on the other hand, been the product and prerogative of the well-to-do upper and middle classes.

It was at this time an essential part of an educated person's curriculum to study music; that is, to learn to sing and to play some instrument or instruments. These were the Viols, the Lute, the Recorders, and, a little later, the Hautboy and Flute. The more well-to-do kept a band of musicians permanently employed as members of the household; and music was played during and after meals. One can still see in old houses and palaces the huge refectories, or banqueting-halls, with their musicians' galleries at one end. From time to time a meal would be interrupted with a dance, just as to-day we have our *diners-dansants*. Nowadays, of course, fashions have changed somewhat: instead of discoursing sweet, gentle Ayres, Pavans and Galliards as a soothing aid to digestion, we have blaring and dyspeptic Swing Music in our restaurants, so designed that it is impossible to hear oneself speak without shouting, and, when shouting, impossible to hear the music. Contemplation and Emotional Experience. . . .

It will have occurred to the reader that the advent of this pleasure-music entailed a radically different attitude on the part of musicians and people generally. Up to this point, I repeat, music was designed for a definite occasion, a ceremony or a ritual. Now we have music to be listened to as music and for the pleasure of the thing. Entertainment-music now came thick and fast. Masques, operas, part-songs, music for little orchestras were now being produced and consumed in increasing quantities. The day when a Consort of instruments was to turn into a Concert was not far distant.

In London the first Concerts open to the public were given by a certain John Bannister between 1672 and 1678. They were held at his house in Whitefriars, Fleet Street, daily at four in the afternoon, and the price of admittance was one shilling. A little later, Thos. Britton, described as " the small-coal man," gave public subscription concerts at his house in Clerkenwell. The subscription was ten shillings a year. Then arose several concert-giving societies, among which many readers will recognise the name of Salomon, who commissioned Haydn to write symphonies for them. This was in the last decade of the eighteenth century. The Royal Philharmonic Society was founded in 1813. August Manns started his concerts at the Crystal Palace. Jullien, mentioned above (page 82), founded the Promenade Concerts at Covent Garden. The Queen's Hall Concerts, the Richter Concerts, the Broadwood Concerts and many more grew up. Music had become a solemn business. Music was itself the Ritual. Philosophical interpretations of music were expounded. People were unable to listen to a Symphony without asking What It Was About. There were those who professed to hear in the opening notes of some great work Fate Knocking on the Door. Others again—or perhaps they were the same people—descried visions of Moonlight when listening to a Sonata. An entirely new trade of analytical dissection of not only music but of the unfortunate composer came into being and flourished. This New or Higher Criticism professed to take into account every most private detail of a composer's life and relate it to this or that work of his. Beethoven, it was found, owed the rent for three weeks in April 1802. Ah, said the knowing ones, his preoccupation with internal spiritual things can be seen to date from that moment.

This was indeed Emotion. But what, the reader will ask with me, had happened to Contemplation? Frankly, I don't know. For some time before and for a while after the turn of the last century people seemed largely to have lost sight of the idea of music. How did we define Music at the beginning of this book? "Music," we said, "is movement of sound, consisting of rhythmical and metrical patterns." It is, we agreed, the interplay of these patterns as apprehended by the ear that gives one pleasure. How, then, had these anti-musical accretions of the so-called philosophical import of music grown up? And why were people told that unless they adopted this attitude to music it was impossible truly to appreciate it? To answer these questions we must go back a bit.

If you consider the folding chart again you will notice that the centre of musical activity has from time to time shifted from one country to another. I do not wish at this point to anticipate the Section on the Genesis of Music. It will be sufficient for our purpose of the moment to begin by looking at what was happening during the period we are discussing: the fifteenth to sixteenth centuries. From the Netherlands the emphasis moved to Italy, thence to Germany. The English School arose about 1520 or so and persisted to about 1760, our one important composer at that time being Arne, who wrote *Rule, Britannia.* (This, to give a topical touch, was first performed at Cliveden, by the way.) It will be seen further that although the Italian output did not diminish in quantity or importance right up to Puccini (1858–1924), an immense musical activity had sprung up in Germany. In the last century music-publishing became a vigorous enterprise. Big businesses were built up: Peters, Breitkopf and Härtel, Schott, Augener, Novello, Chappell, Durand and many other music-publishing houses were founded. Music was in free circulation. It was easily accessible. At the same time railways were being built; steamships came into being. Artists could travel with comparative ease. England was flooded with Continental music and musicians. Her own slender product had been stamped out by the influx of Italian opera and Händel combined. For any English artist to get a hearing at all he or she had to adopt a foreign name.

The rise of industrialism had so absorbed the attention of the only class of people who had the means to indulge themselves in cultured activity, that serious interest in music, which was contemptuously described as an " uneconomic proposition," declined. It became a matter of mere fashion among the old aristocracy, who had as yet been untouched by the novel taint of industrialism, to " patronise the arts." The artist became a paid servant, who was compelled by economic necessity to purvey the kind of art that was acceptable to his masters, or to accept the alternative of " starving in a garret " as the price of his artistic integrity. All of this will be dealt with more fully later on.

Now all this, though seeming to have taken us a long way from our line of inquiry, is relevant, indeed essential, to our understanding of the changed attitude to music in the last century. As has been said above, concerts of music had become rituals in themselves. It is evident to me that mankind needs rituals. When the old rituals fell into disrepute in the Age of Reason, man, the rationalist, made of music (among other things) a ritual. Moreover, he built around music an entire mythology. The source of this curious phenomenon was, as might be expected, Germany, the home of philosophy, metaphysics, *Sturm und Drang* * and many other queer things.

It was, then, the efflorescence of philosophy and metaphysics in Germany to which can be attributed this new and strange approach to music.

* The " Stürmer und Dränger " were the poets of the German Stress Period (1770–1784).

I will abandon this problem for the moment, and retur
to a final consideration of Contemplation and Emotion:
Experience from which we have wandered a good way.
do not propose to examine the music itself in any detail a
the moment. That must wait until the next Section.

I have shown, then, how this new attitude to music gre\
up. People went to concerts to enjoy and, ultimately, t
destroy music. At this point a most curious thing happened

It will have been clear that in earlier times music wa
designed, one may say, to be evocative of deep feelings
whether of worship, thanksgiving or what not. And, in fact
one is forced to believe that people took a very serious par
in these rituals and celebrations. People were actuall\
moved to fervour, and expressed it in song and dance. Bu'
although it might be shown that for a time at least the ne\
pleasure-music was simpler in intention, less profound, shal
we say, it rapidly increased in complexity again; moreover
it cannot be said that at any time there were no composer\
of deeply evocative music. The simplicity of a Purcell (1658–
1695) was a simplicity of texture. We of to-day find it as
capable of moving us emotionally as the devotional music of,
say, Palestrina (1525–1594). But now people began going to
concerts. They sit and listen to music. And how they sit!
Those who respond to the music are inhibited from expressing their response. A tapping toe, the smothered bodily responses, the expression of intellectual stimulation, are frowned
on and even, in this politest of countries, hissed. And rightly
so. There is nothing more disturbing than a sensitive neighbour at a concert who expresses, however inadequately, his
reactions to the music. Consequently, these new devotional
exercises of the concert hall are very secret and private
manifestations. It is with difficulty that those sensitive to
the music can contain themselves. I often think that hab-
itual concert-going eventually inhibits the response altogether.
Certainly one's fellow-listeners look miserable enough. It is
interesting to speculate as to whether these discomforts of
the concert hall are compensated by the canned music provided by a much harassed B.B.C., which enables music to be
heard in the privacy of the home, where one can, if so minded,
dance in the nude in front of a mirror like the poet Swinburne.

It is evident that this aspect of music, that is, its enjoyment,
is in a most unsatisfactory position to-day. And the paradoxical part of it is that music itself is undoubtedly at a

higher level of perfection than ever before. By this I mean not that this or that work by a contemporary composer is ' better " (whatever that might mean) than music written at any other period. It is meaningless to say that a string quartet by Webern (*b.* 1883) is either better or worse than a string quartet by Beethoven (1770–1827). Each may be perfect music in its way and of its kind. In talking of the level of perfection of music to-day, I mean that music is being written of an importance and significance equal to the greatest periods of the past; that, moreover, it is more readily accessible in the printed and audible forms (the concert room, the gramophone, the radio) than ever before; that the standard of performance is, from the evidence available, considerably higher than has obtained in past history; and that the audiences are, on the whole, willing, eager and discriminating listeners.

And at that we must leave the Contemplation and Emotional Experience of music, and pass on to other things.

### (iii) MUSIC-DRAMA AND OPERA

Related to the foregoing instances of Occasions for Music —Celebration and Ritual, Contemplation and Emotional Experience—are those dramatic representations of which music is an integral part. These have formed a very important part of mankind's æsthetic activities, connected originally with magic and religious manifestations and later developing into purely secular entertainment.

It must be realised that dramatic representation of various religious and quasi-religious rites has been a feature of devotional exercises all over the world. We can but glance at some European examples of these in a book of this scope.

The European tradition grew mainly out of the ancient Greek Dionysiac Festivals, which later were grafted on to the Christian Church. The Greek dithyramb was the essence of these rites of Dionysos, who was identical with the Egyptian Osiris in his attributes and legendary life: the parthenogenetic birth, the pre-ordained immolation and final resurrection, all attributed to the later Christ. The mysterious Goat Song, or *tragôidia,* of the Greek drama is worthy of mention in this further example of dramatised song and dance.

In post-Christian times the Mithraic ritual in connection with December 25 appears along with the Teutonic legend of the Egg of Eostretide at Easter. There were the " Winchester tropes " in the ninth century A.D., the " Mysteries " of France in the eleventh century, and the English Miracle Plays and Moralities of the twelfth century, which were borrowed from France. All of these were religious or quasi-religious rites of which music, dancing and singing formed an essential part.

Mention has already been made of the appearance of legitimate Opera in the seventeenth century. The actual prototype of Dramma per la Musica was a representation of the classical story of *Euridice* by Peri (1561–1633). Thereafter, as the sacred drama declined, Opera developed through Monteverde (1567–1643), Cavalli (1600–1676), Lully (1632–1687), Alessandro Scarlatti (1658–1725), Purcell (1658–1695), Reinhard Keiser (1673–1739)—the first Singspiel to be publicly performed in German was Johann Theile's *Adam und Eva* in 1678—Händel (1685–1759), Pergolesi (1710–1735), Arne (1710–1778), Gluck (1714–1787), Mozart (1756–1791), Beethoven (1770–1827), Weber (1786–1826), Meyerbeer (1791–1864), Rossini (1792–1868), Verdi (1813–1901), Wagner (1813–1883) and so down to our own day. This catalogue of names is, the reader will observe, arranged chronologically. They are but sample names out of the many which have made important contributions to the art of opera, whose centre of gravity has shifted from one country to another as time has passed.

In the next Section (p. 98) a rather more detailed discussion of Opera will be embarked on. At the moment it is sufficient to have mentioned it in connection with Occasions for Music.*

(iv) LIGHTER FORMS: INCIDENTAL AND DANCE

We will now turn to two other most important functions of music: Incidental Music and Dance Music.

In a sense it can be said that music for religious services and other rituals and celebrations is incidental. But the usual connotation of the term Incidental is music which from time to time accompanies the action of a play, where musical occasions are portrayed on the stage, as distinct from the music of operas and such-like where the music is an integral part of the entertainment.

Incidental Music as such would seem to be of comparatively late origin. In the first instance, as has already been shown,

---

* The interested reader is referred to Professor Dent's *Opera* (Pelican Books Ltd.), for a scholarly and most readable survey of the subject which is necessarily more complete than the cursory outline which is all that has been attempted here.

94

music and drama were one. Just as music on the one hand separated itself from ritual and began to lead an independent life of its own, so too did drama. Examples can be found of a musical work with spoken passages interpolated just as dramatic pieces of a certain period begin to have what is called Incidental Music. The two developments are parallel.

Incidental Music, then, consists of preludes and interludes, marches, dances and songs. A very few examples will suffice to illustrate this.

There was the Incidental Music to Milton's *Comus* by Henry Lawes (1600–1662); and composers such as Matthew Locke (1630–1677) and Christopher Gibbons (1615–1676) wrote a lot of Incidental Music to plays now mostly forgotten. There were the Theatre Ayres of Purcell (1658–1695), the Incidental Music to *Egmont* [46] and *Leonora Prohaska* by Beethoven (1770–1827), to *A Midsummer Night's Dream* [47] by Mendelssohn (1809–1847), and to *L'Arlésienne* [42] by Bizet (1838–1875), and in our own day Delius (1863–1934) has written Incidental Music to Flecker's *Hassan* [48]. And so on.

Independently of all this the Dance emancipated itself from ritual in the same way. Mention has already been made of some dance forms in the Section on Musical Forms.

Dances originally were directly representational. And since the things they represented were mainly concerned with fertility rites and such-like they were what we nowadays would call lascivious in character. It was only later that they achieved a degree of formalisation and stylisation. Nevertheless the fact remains that a basis of sexual symbolism is shown more or less clearly in every existing dance; must be so, in the nature of things.

The more puritan elements in society have from time to time raised outcries and succeeded in modifying certain elements of the dance. As already mentioned on page 32, the stately Pavan was at one time condemned for its lascivious character. Likewise the Sarabande, which we now know only as a slow and rather stiff formal dance, was originally of such a character that Mariana (1536–1623), writing in a *Treatise against Public Amusements,* inveighed against it as follows: " Entre las otras invenciones ha salido estos años un baile y cantar tan lacivo en las palabras, tan feo en las meneos, que basta para pegar fuego aun á las personas muy honestas." (Amongst other inventions there has appeared during late years a dance and song, so lascivious in its words, so ugly in its movements, that it is enough to inflame even very modest people.) Under Philip II of Spain, that gastronomic recluse, this dance was altogether suppressed. But nowadays the only examples familiar to us are the staid movements of considerable gravity in the Suites of Bach and his contemporaries.

Dancing, albeit it retained vestiges of its original ritual character among the common people, became an important social activity, which is retained to this day. Further mention of this, also, must be postponed to a later Section.

\*       \*       \*

Occasions for Music thus fall into four distinct categories: Celebration and Ritual, Contemplation and Emotional Experience, Music-drama and Opera, and the lighter forms such as Incidental Music and the Dance.

# VI

## RECAPITULATION

BEFORE we proceed farther I wish to interpolate here a very brief Recapitulation of the foregoing.

The Physical Basis of Music resides in a recurring series of rhythmical, metrical and melodic patterns, which, apprehended by the ear, are capable of inducing emotional and intellectual, in short æsthetic, reactions in the listener. These fundamental principles can be dissected up to a point; this or that work can be shown to display the prerequisites as laid down in doctrinaire form by theoreticians. But in so doing one runs the grave danger of killing the very thing one loves by thus sterilising the life out of that very vital thing, Music.

The Nature of Musical Thought is less susceptible to factual analysis, being rooted in fantasy and the unconscious mind of the composer, upon which an acquired technique necessary for the clear expression of his ideas is superimposed.

For a composer to cast his musical thoughts into a recognised or recognisable mould or form is as essential as is the grammar and syntax of everyday speech. A conglomeration of sounds, no matter how beautiful in themselves, cannot adequately convey to the listener "musical sense" unless there is an apprehensible inner logic perceptible.

Musical ideas in Europe and the Americas are transcribed in a system of notation laid down as early as the tenth century by Guido d'Arezzo, who evolved the principle of a system of lines and spaces on which various symbols are written, these symbols conveying to the executive musician an approximation to the composer's intentions. This system is imperfect, even when supplemented by verbal directions. There is no absolute standard of speed in notation. A crotchet or a quaver may be played at any conceivable speed within the limits of, say, 56 to 212 to the minute. The actual speed in performance relies partly on the verbal directions at the beginning of the piece of music, such as Quick, Slow, etc. But in the main the composer has to rely on the musicianship of the performer for an adequate rendering of his music.

The instruments on which music of to-day is performed vary in antiquity. There are at present about twenty-five different kinds of such instruments in use, excluding the varieties of percussion instruments. Each of these twenty-five instruments has its imperfections and limitations; each requires a considerable degree of technical skill as well as a high standard of what one can only call intuitive musicianship on the part of the player.

This formidable array of preliminaries is devoted to music for various occasions. The chief of these has always been Celebration and Ritual. At a later period in the history of the art came the first emancipation when music was played or sung for its own sake: Contemplation and Emotional Experience. Allied to these occasions are Music-drama and Opera, which in their turn also arose out of Celebration and Ritual, becoming fully secularised only within comparatively recent times (the sixteenth century). A parallel development is observable when drama and music begin to lead independent existences of their own and purely musical pieces have spoken passages interpolated just as dramatic pieces have Incidental Music, consisting of preludes, interludes, marches, songs and dances.

# PART II

# THE GENESIS OF MUSIC

THE writing of history is no easy task. To attempt to trace the development of any one particular aspect in isolation from its social context leads inevitably to gross errors, as was shown in the section on The Nature of Musical Thought. On the other hand, to take into account all the relevant factors demands not only a considerable scholarly equipment, but requires more detailed treatment than can be accorded to it in a book of this scope. Thus there can be no adequate discussion of many important aspects of musical history, such as developments of musical forms and orchestration, etc.

I propose, therefore, to give no more than a brief conspectus of the salient features of European music. To do this, a convenient method appears to be to examine the main trends of European music to-day, and to trace retrospectively the antecedent causes which produced them.

## (i) THE CONTEMPORARY SCENE (1943–c. 1910)

The turbulent times in which we are now living are reflected in much of the music that is produced to-day. This is what might be expected. Since it is manifest that society is in a constant state of flux, with an established social system which in one phase is progressively growing and expanding; at a later phase has reached a certain degree of stability; and finally passes into decay, in order to give way to a new progressive system; so, too, do we find analogous movements in music and the arts generally.

An interesting phenomenon, which will be examined later in some detail (see Section VIII, " The Great Schism ") is the existing three-fold cleavage between Art-Music, Folk-Music and Commercialised Music.

The Art-Music (" high-brow ") which has been produced during these last few years makes its appeal to a circle of cognoscenti, which, under capitalism, is steadily diminishing numerically. It tends to be of a highly complex, remote and ethereal quality; and ultimately becomes a completely private language. In its extremest forms it would seem to be fully understood only by the composer himself. A parallel development can be seen in the writings of James Joyce. This phenomenon can be explained, I suggest, by the rejection of the harshness, discomforts and crudities of the external world acting on sensitive people who choose thus to escape and to cut themselves off from the living people. We will return to this kind of music in a moment.

The Folk-Music of to-day is, in the main, the product of the American depressed classes; particularly of the Negroes of the Southern United States. It is noticeable that the highly industrialised parts of the world are barren of such Folk-music.

The town-dwellers have for their musical diet Commercialised Jazz. This product of Tin-Pan Alley is based on the (American) Folk-music which the ruling classes have appropriated from the people. The result is that the form and superficial trappings of style are all that is left; so that it emerges as an anæsthetic, a dope, building dream-worlds of sugary and maudlin romance which in fact deflect people's attention from the realities of the external world. It owes much of its appeal to intensive advertisement (" song-plugging " on the radio) which bludgeons people into acceptance of the metronomic drum-beats and sterile four-square rhythms. There are, however, undoubted reasons other than advertising by repetition for the singular hold which this social product has on the community. These reasons are to be found in the characteristics which are peculiar to the music.

Firstly: the unbroken rhythmical monotony of sixteen, thirty-two or occasionally forty-eight beats, which persist with the inflexibility of a machine, tends to induce in the listener a state akin to hypnosis.

Secondly: the thematic material consists of two or three trite musical formulæ * (the most frequent being tonic-sub-dominant-dominant-tonic) which are basically as impossible to forget as they are, in their embroidered forms, to remember.

---

\* The fact that any of these dance " numbers " can be conveniently sustained by the two basic and most elementary chords at the disposal of the least accomplished amateur strummer on the ukulele, or other similar instrument, clearly demonstrates the extremely narrow confines of these musical formulæ.

Thirdly: the suggestive bodily movements which are evoked by this music demonstrate its strong erotic appeal.

Fourthly: the words sung are invariably either nostalgic, the singer expressing a wish to be somewhere other than he or she is at the moment; or otherwise escapist, by pretending that the love-object is a baby, an angel, a strong hero, or, in fact, anything but the actuality. (See further "The Great Schism," Section VIII.)

In contrast to this three-fold cleavage in the music of the capitalist world, is a new development in the Soviet Union. Here, manifestly, is a social order which, having abolished privileged classes, is on the way to a classless society. As might be expected, therefore, we find in the music of the U.S.S.R. a flourishing Art-Music, co-existing quite amicably with true Popular Music. This popular music is designed primarily to make a mass-appeal, and is suitable for what we in this country call "community-singing," demonstrations and the like. The roots of this music appear to be in the Folk-music indigenous to the various nationalities which comprise the U.S.S.R.

With regard to Art-Music in the U.S.S.R., the foremost composer, in my opinion, is Prokofiev (b. 1891). He left Russia in 1918, and established for himself a world-wide reputation as composer and pianist. In 1933, at the invitation of the Soviet Government, he returned to the U.S.S.R., where he has been ever since. His considerable output includes symphonies and piano concertos. But in the main his interest lies in theatre-music. The reader is recommended to hear the Third Piano Concerto [49] and the delightful children's entertainment, *Peter and the Wolf* [49].

Shostakovich (b. 1906) displays a very considerable talent, which has expressed itself in music of every form [50]. There are also composers such as Maximilian Steinberg (b. 1883), who, incidentally, taught Shostakovich; Khachaturian (b. 1904) [51] and others whose music is not readily accessible in this country.

Dunayevsky (b. 1900) is perhaps the best-known composer of Soviet Popular Music [52].

I do not propose to discuss Soviet music critically with the attention it undoubtedly deserves, beyond saying that it is unquestionably animated and vital in outlook, although one may reasonably say that it is as yet immature in many respects. But it would be a mistake to apply the standards of European-capitalist society, with its long traditions of differing class-cultures, to music composed in and for a young Socialist State.

The reader must be content with these brief remarks, and allow me to return to the Art-music which is our own social product.

Owing to the facility of international communications, a factor which was touched on in a preceding Section, one derives the impression that more music is being written than at any other period in the world's history. How true this is is hard to estimate. It has always been true that the bulk of music composed has been forgotten owing to its mediocrity. Only the really outstanding works of any generation have been perpetuated. The same doubtless holds good to-day. The difference is that any music written now has to be exceedingly bad of its kind not to achieve some performance somewhere. And that Somewhere is, more often than not, one of the Radio Corporations of the world.

Consequently, although there is no doubt that there is an unparalleled consumption of music to-day, it may be an entirely false idea that there is an unusual productive activity among the younger composers.

In fact, to take the last ten years or so as a moment in time, the very reverse may be true. For one has to take into account the special case of Germany. What is happening in the strictly contemporary scene in Germany is difficult to say. It has been the policy of the German Government to kill, imprison or exile all composers (among other artists, scientists and the like) who were the most highly esteemed by the rest of the world. It would appear that creative musical activity is for the moment at a standstill. (Schönberg left Berlin for the United States voluntarily some years ago; Berg is dead; Hindemith is in the United States; and no one seems to know what has happened to Webern, who was last heard of still in Vienna (November 1939).)

Going back to the older generation, then, we find three main streams in musical development. It is not that it is difficult to disentangle these various currents. But it is difficult to present them with an appearance of simultaneity. Of necessity they must be treated of one by one. I am not writing triple invertible counterpoint now, with all my themes drawn together in a grand *stretto*.

First of all let us recall to mind a very important physical fact about music; namely, the tuning of our scale in the Mean Temperament. It was pointed out (page 42) that this Mean Temperament reduced to practical absurdity the notion that D flat is a different note from C sharp. The theoretical difference has become a fiction. (In parenthesis, it must be admitted that this difference persists, and persists audibly, on stringed instruments.) Arising out of a realistic attitude to this fact is the disappearance of the ancient predominance of one note, formerly called the Key-note, or Tonic, over any other. Similarly there is no-reason other than ingrained habit for allowing any note any degree of precedence over another.

Music, it is held by this school of thought, must henceforth be what is called Atonal—without a tonal centre, or recurring focal point.

What is Tonality?

In a few words it may be called a particular Musical Alphabet. As was explained earlier in this book, although the octave is divided into twelve equal parts, composers have not, as a rule, employed the full resources of the entire Chromatic Scale. They limit themselves to a scale consisting of eight, five or some other small number of notes.* The reason for this was indicated on page 17. Therefore, as long as a piece of music built on one scale (written in one key, as we say) in a general way confines itself to the notes of that scale (or key), it is said to stand in the key of C major, A minor or whatever it may be. This is its Tonality. One of the ways in which composers have sought to introduce a greater variety into their music has been to modulate from one key to another by means of some pivotal point where the inner harmonic sense enables an easy transition to be effected. During the course of an extended movement the music may modulate through a succession of half a dozen keys or more and yet retain the basis of true Tonality. The transitions, or Modulations, from one key to another are explicit and clearly stated.

An indispensable feature of Tonal music is the Cadence, which may be likened to a species of punctuation. There is

---

* Any History of Painting will tell you that painters habitually limit the number of pigments on their palettes. No painter uses the entire resources of pigment at one time. This is mentioned as an analogy to the composer's self-imposed limitations of his tonal vocabulary.

a series of such conventional and quasi-conventional Cadences which in effect are moments of harmonic repose, whereby the music returns from modulatory excursions to the dead-centre of its particular key, and thus enables the composer to keep his Tonality in his head and his audience their feet on the ground.

I can best demonstrate this to those readers who possess a piano with two examples, the first simple, the second more complicated.

Ex. 7

In this instance it will be seen that the introduction of one note, F natural, leads from the key of G major into the key of C major, where the rest of the passage remains. (The scale of C major consisting entirely of the "white notes" on the piano, F sharp is outside it.)

Ex. 8

In this second example the second, third and fourth chords provide a series of pivotal points leading finally to E flat major. This elementary example of free and frequent modulation imparts the characteristic of restless Tonality associated with Fauré (1845–1924), and, as we shall see later, with Wolf (1860–1903) and Reger (1873–1916) in Germany still more.

Having, as I hope, got clear in our minds what Tonality is, we can now go on to discuss Atonality.

As we said above, the logical outcome of the Mean Temperament was the abandonment of any sense of a Key-note, or recurring focal point, together with fixed Tonality.

On this theoretical basis of Atonality, which is as good as any other theoretical basis that has obtained in the past, an elaborate structure of musical science has been built.

Arnold Schönberg (b. 1874) is the architect of this supremely logical edifice. His prototype may be found in Josquin des Prés (1445–1521), the Netherlands composer and theoretician, out of whose work arose the whole Italian and German Schools of Polyphony, about which we will talk later.

Already from Schönberg's teachings have sprung at least two composers before whom even the most reactionary of critics bows as to a master. These are Anton Webern (b. 1883) and Alban Berg (1885–1936). It is unfortunate that of the three, Berg and Webern are the only ones whose representative work is available on gramophone records. The recording of Webern's String Trio [53], opus 20 (erroneously described on the record label as opus 21), is an event of the first importance in the history of recorded music. It is music of rare quality; but, I must warn the reader impatient to rush off to his nearest gramophone dealer, it is not easy to listen to if he has, as is almost inevitable, the Tonic-Dominant pre-possessions of the general run of Europeans. Nevertheless, I advise him to hear this record, and try to put himself in a frame of mind where he is content to allow the magic of the pure beauty of sound to soak into him and flow around him. After several hearings he will surely begin to appreciate the immense musicality of the mind that conceived it. Nevertheless, the fact remains that it is not a work that I would choose for the purpose of introducing the ordinary musical listener to Atonal Music of this variety.

In many ways easier to listen to is the extremely important *Lyric Suite* [54] for String Quartet by Berg.

It is music such as this which has reached the apparent limits of obscurity. It most surely reflects the social attitude of the composer who puts himself as far out of reach of the ordinary run of mankind as is a bunch of grapes for the English working-man at Christmas. In both cases it is 'the social opportunity for appreciation that is lacking.

The second stream of musical activity is represented by its

founder, Paul Hindemith (*b*. 1894). Hindemith also evolved a system which has been called Atonal. But he himself repudiates the word as applied to his music. There is, as he points out, a clearly defined tonal centre, or series of tonal centres, in all his music, which is very personal and differs unmistakably from that of the true atonalists in every respect except one. Schönberg and his followers have in common with Hindemith and his imitators—there is a difference between a follower and an imitator—the use they make of the old strict musical forms. Schönberg and Berg on the one side (more than Webern), and Hindemith on the other, frequently cast their music into Fugues, Passacaglias and the like. Hindemith's music is entirely contrapuntal in the same sense that Bach's music is; the music of the atonalists is frequently enriched with pure harmonic embellishment.

The music of Hindemith is considerably more ingratiating and easy on the ear than that of the atonalists proper. This is particularly true of his middle period, the period of the two full-scale operas, the Second Viola Concerto, etc. Latterly, however, it appears to me that he has become dry and academic. The exuberant buoyancy of his quick movements has been displaced by a mechanical dullness; and the elegant tenderness of his slow movements by contrapuntal devices which appear barren of significance or charm. Unfortunately, the only recorded works of Hindemith now available are the Symphony [55], the Second String Trio [56] and a trifling Duet for Viola and 'Cello [57] which he wrote specially for the Columbia History of Music. The early recording of his delightful Third String Quartet is now withdrawn.

Co-existing with these developments is Igor Stravinsky (*b*. 1882), whose music shows the persistence of tonality; there are only three works of his in which he has abandoned a tonality which is always definite enough to need a key-signature.* There is a wide choice of works by Stravinsky recorded by various companies [58]. Every one of his works is so individual that I would hesitate to pick out any one and say that it was absolutely representative. I have no space here to write a monograph on the artistic development of this astonishing artist, who is never content to say a thing twice

* If a piece is written in the key of G major, the note F sharp will constantly recur—never F natural, always F sharp. To save everyone time and trouble the piece accordingly is prefaced by the key-signature of One Sharp—F sharp.

because it was good the first time. Always he seeks new paths for expression, new vehicles for his ideas.

Here, too, we find a degeneracy. The individual features which were so distinctive and satisfying by reason of their *rightness* have become enfeebled *clichés* and, one suspects, have developed into an exploitation of the bizarre for its own sake.

These three schools of contemporary music are the main streams in musical thought to-day. The Schönberg School with its doctrinaire system of Atonality; Hindemith with his essentially contrapuntal music with, as one might say, a complex of tonal centres; and Stravinsky, who still adheres to a fixed tonality. Their different kinds of music must be left to speak for themselves—as, indeed, I feel all music should. Ultimately, as I said earlier in this book, either you like it or you don't. If you don't, it does not matter to anyone; except in so far as you are the poorer for not being able for this or that reason to appreciate one more thing. Certain it is that no amount of " explanation " will induce you to like certain music, any more than a lecture on dietetics makes you like food that your palate rejects. The most one can say is that, if you are sufficiently interested, you should hear it. And hear it again and again and again.

Now from what are these three kinds of music derived, the reader will be asking? We must postpone the answers—for there are several—for the moment. All I can say at this stage in the exposition of my history is that Schönberg derives from the German " Romantics," who will be treated of presently; Hindemith from the German " Classics " (see (iv) (*b*) below); and Stravinsky from the Great Russians (see (iii) below).

I have purposely and of necessity given considerable space to this review of the Contemporary Scene. But from now on I am compelled drastically to condense the alarming quantity of material which properly requires extended treatment.

### (ii) " THE ROMANTICS "

### (*a*) The French (1937–c. 1827)

There is an arbitrary classification of music current among musicians into " Classical " and " Romantic." Like all labels, these have their advantages and their drawbacks. A label is a convenient thing from many points of view. One is apt to believe that if only one can pin down something by giving it a label, one has somehow come nearer to "the truth." I myself have found this notion frequently misleading, as in the present instance. It is, no doubt, convenient on occasion to be able to label a person Socialist or Conservative. But many Socialists are conservative in some things just as many Conservatives are socialist in some things. The convenience of a label resides in the fact that it tells you something about a person or thing, but the drawback is that it doesn't tell you everything. Thus a composer generally regarded as Romantic may in some respects be Classical.

In any case, it is exceedingly hard to give a working definition of either. Under the heading Classical my dictionary says: "Learned in the Classics, relating to the Classics, conforming to the rules or models of Greek or Latin antiquity (of literature), *hence opposite to Romantic*" (my italics). Turning to Romantic, I find an astonishing congeries of meanings: "Of the nature of or having the qualities of romance in respect of form or content. Characterised by the subordination of form to a theme, and by imagination and passion. Of a fabulous or fictitious character; having no foundation in fact. Imaginary; purely ideal, etc." (*Oxford English Dictionary*.)

From this maze one may extract this: that the Romantic artist in this sense is a type which tends to derive the Form from the Content; and the Classical artist is the opposite.

To this must be added further qualities, qualities of *social outlook*. The Romantic tends towards an exaltation of the individual, towards an escape from reality, towards a purely subjective attitude: he builds dream-worlds of the imagined charms of the idealised past, such as the lamented age of chivalry, the noble sagas of the Irish Kings, or legends of mythological antiquity; conveniently disregarding the extreme personal hazards of ancient days, and the lack of the most elementary of civilised amenities such as electric light and indoor sanitation.

It is less easy to arrive at a closer definition of the Classical composer, as opposed to his Romantic counterpart. Merely to state his attitude in terms of opposition to that of the Romantic is inadequate and even misleading; for it would be in no sense true to suggest that he dwells lovingly on the beauties of gas-works and sewers. I incline to the general statement that the Classical composer has an attitude of *courageous social-realism.* He achieves the fulfilment of his individuality by the paradoxical means of identifying himself with the social world at large.

The matter is further complicated by the fact, indicated above, that the two types do not conveniently fit into one category or the other. But two clearly opposed examples may clarify this: Mozart the Classical, Wagner the Romantic. With Mozart the formal structure in which he casts his ideas plays an integral and decisive part in the ideas themselves. With Wagner the importance of the germ-idea, the isolated moment of sound, is stressed; and out of the material the musical form grows and develops. It may justifiably be said that only too often it swells unmanageably and boils over until the audience is swamped in an inchoate and amorphous welter.

With Maurice Ravel (1875–1937) the last trickle of French Romanticism dried up. In addition to the recorded works already mentioned (*Daphnis and Chloe* [25] and *The Enchanted Flute* [59] from Schéhérazade), the reader is referred to the String Quartet [60] and the lovely early piano piece *Jeux d'Eau* [61].

The apex of the French Romantics was Claude Debussy (1862–1918). The common forefather of both was Gabriel Fauré (1845–1924). Debussy's *L'Après-Midi d'un Faune* [24] has already been cited. There are in addition numerous piano pieces, such as the two books of Preludes and the little-known Studies [62], which will delight every listener.

Behind Ravel and Debussy is an array of names of the French Romantics, many of whom are not in vogue at the moment, but whose intrinsic qualities will reassert themselves in time. Gabriel Fauré (1845–1924), Jules Massenet (1842–1912), Alexis Emmanuel Chabrier (1841–1894) are among them. Nor must one forget Erik Satie (1866–1925), contemporary with Debussy, whose formative influence was felt outside the music of his own country. To conclude the list, let us mention Georges Bizet (1838–1875), César Franck (1822–1890), and the progenitor of them all, Hector Berlioz (1803–1869).

So far as it is possible to consider the music of these French Romantics under a single heading, it may be said that it is characterised by a lightness and sparkle, a directness of approach and of expression, which are qualities peculiar to the genius of the French in all their manifestations. This lightness is not levity nor mere emptiness. It is an airy buoyancy which is as unmistakably French as is their language.

That singular figure Erik Satie (1866-1925) was among the first to take more than an antiquarian interest in ancient music of the kind popularly called Gregorian Chant (although Pope Gregory had nothing to do with it at all). He revived the simplicity of this ancient mode of writing music by basing many of his own works directly on the old Church Modes * and by employing a harmonic scheme of bare fourths and fifths in place of the discordant lusciousness of thirds and sixths which had held sway for four centuries. Satie's whimsicality was a great obstacle to his acceptance by the general musical public as a serious composer. But it would be a mistake to assess his worth only by these eccentricities. His truly musical influence was a very real and important thing, although he himself remained in poverty and obscurity for most of his life. He may be said to have heralded the movement known as Neo-Classical, which assumed a considerable prominence after the last war. (Although Saint-Saëns must not be overlooked in this connection. There is at least one most peculiar " Neo-Classical " work of his, the Septet for string quartet, double-bass, trumpet and piano, which for sheer perversity outmatches the most precious of the younger French composers.)

Gabriel Fauré (1845-1924) was a composer of great distinction and real refinement. Among other features that his music possesses is a remarkable harmonic richness with which is associated kaleidoscopic tonality-sequences. Unfortunately no important mature work appears to be available on the gramophone.

There is no space at my disposal for dealing with the other representatives of the French Romantics as I should wish. It must suffice to instance typical examples so that the listener can hear for himself the kind of music they wrote. All I can hope to do is to attempt to relate this with the main stream of musical development.

I will therefore typify the remaining French Romantics as follows: Massenet (1842-1912) can be represented by " En fermant les yeux " from *Manon* [63]; Chabrier (1841-1894) by *Spanish Rhapsody* [64]; Bizet (1838-1875) by *L'Arlésienne* [42]; Franck (1822-1890) by *Prelude, Chorale and Fugue* [65];

* See page 19.

and Berlioz (1803–1869) by the *Symphonie Fantastique* [38] and the *Carnaval Romain* [41], already mentioned.

We cannot, however, afford to dismiss Berlioz so briefly As with most great composers, an immense controversy (which, by the way, is not yet dead) has raged over and around him for close on a hundred years. His music has the vital and dynamic urge to it that still can disconcert listeners to-day by the genius for the bizarre and unexpected which it betrays. His orchestration was startling in its innovations and richness. The influence he exerted over his followers, more even than over his contemporaries, was immense. Liszt (1811–1886), that other great fertiliser of musical genius, owed much to him, as did Wagner (1813–1883). These two recorded examples of his works must suffice for the listener to draw his own conclusions as to the ultimate worth of the progenitor of the French Romantics.

A parenthesis must be made here, since it is outside the scope of this book to provide a proper context, for mention of Chopin (1810–1849), Polish son of a French-born father. He was a virtuoso composer (if I may use the expression) for the piano; and his influence on music for that instrument is certainly comparable to that exerted by his friends Liszt (1811–1886) and Schumann (1810–1856), and may be held by some to be even greater.

### (b) *The German* (1943–*c.* 1800)

The German Romantics present a very different picture. Their latest manifestation in the Schönberg School is one of those bewildering instances of the inadequacy of labels. It is true to say that Alban Berg was a Romantic. It is also true to say that he was a Classical composer. In so far as he was a Romantic he presents as perfect an example of that approach to his art as can well be found in modern times: the surging harmonic richness, the use of small motives and patterns of sound to build up his edifice, the choice of subject for his operatic works. On the other hand, he also, and in the same works, employs the Classical approach of fitting his material to the strict musical forms of the Passacaglia, the Fugue and so on. And yet withal he contrives to achieve an integration which in no way produces a sense of incongruity such as one might expect to arise from this duality. The same may be said of Webern. I should be hard put to it to ascribe to either this or that emphasis. To sum up, I should say that

Schönberg, Webern and Berg achieve a synthesis of the Romantic and the Classical hitherto unknown in the history of music.

We turn now to the immediate forefathers of the Schönberg School. The period of the German Romantic School covers about a hundred-and-fifty years—from the present-day representatives to about 1800. During this time a lot happened.

First: Reger (1873–1911), a composer of great historical significance. His music displays an astounding proliferation, a wild and seemingly ungovernable exfoliation, which obscures itself in penumbrous harmonic implications. Besides this, there is in his music a most important and significant thing: his tonality. It is chaotic. Key-signatures change every few bars, so that it is impossible for the listener to unravel the maze of kaleidoscopic changes. Bewilderment and exhaustion rapidly set in. With infinite skill one arrives at, say, C sharp, only to find the composer leaving it as if it were D flat. An immense harmonic and melodic subtlety is built up on these lines, a subtlety so elusive that there are many moments when it is obvious that the composer himself gets entangled in his own ingenuity of tortuous thought and no longer knows what he is doing. It was this chaos which was systematised by Schönberg. Reger was feeling his way to it, but was not big enough—or the times were not ripe— to sweep aside the tonal prejudices to which he was heir and co-ordinate on a rational basis the evident disappearance of Tonality which he sensed but could not formulate.

A parallel development was going on in France at about the same time, as has already been hinted, with Fauré, thirty years older than Reger. With the Frenchman, however, the restless Tonality never became unmanageable. There is about Fauré a refinement and distinction which no German, whatever his virtues, could ever achieve. The reader is recommended to hear Reger's Scherzo from the String Quartet in E flat major, opus 109 [66], to appreciate his importance.

Mahler (1860–1911), who achieved immense fame as a conductor all over the world, was the last representative of the great Viennese tradition of big symphonists, a tradition inherited from Bruckner and Schubert. The time may come when the world will be ready for a revival of his works. They are all conceived on a vast scale. There are nine symphonies, most of them with solo singers and chorus. The

111

Eighth Symphony requires one thousand performers. An example of his music in a small form is accessible on the gramophone: *Ich atmet' einen linden Duft* [67]. It is interesting, by the way, to compare this with the early Schönberg song on the other side of the record from *Das Buch der hängenden Gärten* [68], published a dozen years after the Mahler song just quoted.

The monumental figure of Wagner (1811–1883) dominated his epoch, and still occupies the exclusive attention of many music-lovers to-day, even if he was the progenitor of much that was worthless in the so-called Neo-Wagnerians. I am not suggesting that he is a figure which can or should be disregarded. His music-dramas epitomise the many attempts to weld the three arts of drama, music and decoration into a true unity. And it must be conceded that his was no vain attempt, as has been unkindly suggested, to homogenise oil, beer and water. In any case his music, or quite enough of it, will be so familiar to every reader, whether he likes it or not, that it would be merely redundant to intrude with proffered selections. Wagner's influence is discernible for thirty years after his death in 1883.

I might here interpolate that when considering the German Romantics the first attribute that strikes one is the love of what they call the Kolossal. The glorification of sheer size, bulk, mass and weight has been a particularly German characteristic, especially since 1871, when the Germans became conscious of themselves as a Nation, united by ties of Blood, Race, Language; and with a Mission, a Divine Mission, to impose their Culture on the rest of the unwilling world, which felt not a little frightened (when it was not amused at what seemed to it mere bombast) at this monstrous eruption.

In common with the rest of his countrymen of the period, Wagner was under the spell of the virtue of size. The opening of a Wagner music-drama, say the first three or four hours, is tolerable. But thereafter only the hardiest can survive.

But unquestionably the biggest figure in the nineteenth century was the Hungarian-born Liszt (1811–1886). During his long life his astoundingly fertile brain poured forth music in all forms. He was, among other things, the inventor of the Symphonic Poem, a form which was fastened on by his contemporaries and successors alike. The Symphonic Poem is a development of Programme Music carried to its uttermost extreme.

* * *

It is opportune to touch on this aspect of music here. Reference to its existence was made earlier in this book (page 27), when I promised the reader to deal with it more fully later on.

It has been the subject of much wrangling in the past between those who favour it as an artistic expression and those who insist on its opposite, Absolute Music. Absolute Music has no other object than the realisation of beauty in terms of pure sound. Programme Music, on the other hand, relies considerably for its appeal on literary associations. In the simplest instance a mere label, such as Debussy used for his Piano Preludes, is intended to set the mood of the piece— although it is important to know in this connection that Debussy gave titles to his pieces after they were written and not before. Full-dress Programme Music, however, is altogether more ambitious. A more or less complicated story is attached to the piece. In Strauss's Symphonic Poems *Ein Heldenleben* [69] and *Till Eulenspiegel* [30] the listener is presented with complete biographies illustrated by the music. A wealth of ingenuity is expended by the composer in portraying minute incidents in his heroes' lives. The proper place for this sort of thing is really the cinema.

* * *

To return to Liszt, who began all this: his influence extended to the Russian composers, who were coming into being at that time. He animated Chopin and Berlioz. Wagner and Schumann came under his sway. His prodigies of pianism amazed the world. It is unfortunate that he is to-day generally known only by his lesser works, such as the Hungarian Rhapsodies for piano, which have been "arranged" for every conceivable combination of instruments. But the things by which he will live as a composer are the big symphonic works, the two piano concertos, and the piano sonata.

(A striking parallel with this singular genius came in later times with Busoni (1866–1924), an enigmatic composer, a pianist of fantastic virtuosity, who permeated the musical life of his time in precisely the same way as did Liszt. He is too important a figure not to mention, at the same time difficult to assess as a composer. All the machinery of music is present. There is nothing that that man did not know. Listening to his music one gets carried away by the brilliance of conception and the amazing musical intellect. But every musician of to-day will admit that he remains an enigma. We leave him with a question mark, bracketed with his prototype.)

Both Schumann (1810–1856) and Schubert (1797–1828) contributed notably to chamber music and to the symphony. The former is known chiefly by his piano works, the latter by his superb Lieder. The world would undoubtedly be the poorer without their music; but neither was distinguished as the founder or the apex of any particular school or movement.

Weber (1786–1826) is a figure whose importance can scarcely be exaggerated. His influence touched every sphere of music: orchestration, the development of the variation form, the technique of piano playing, the development of German opera, and, above all, the rich fertility of his new and advanced ideas. In addition to all this, he was a magnificent conductor. There is no space to deal adequately with him here. We must be content with pointing out his greatest achievement: the popularising of native opera in Germany, which up to that time had been overrun by Italian composers and artists. It was not until late in his short life that he achieved the fame he deserved. It was the performance in Berlin of his opera *Der Freischütz* [70], which took him three years to compose, that finally established his fame beyond all question. Thereafter his success was immense wherever he went. Unparalleled acclamation followed the composer, culminating in his visit to London for the production of his opera *Oberon* [71], which had been specially commissioned by Covent Garden Royal Opera House (in parenthesis, imagine a composer being commissioned for a work by that ancient institution to-day); and there he died. A plaque on the house where he stayed while in London may be seen in Portland Place to this day. Among his other activities was the writing of many *pièces d'occasion,* ephemeral music, as the composer well knew, but done with all the craftsmanship and sincerity which he put into his other enduring and more important works. As will be pointed out later in the Section on The Great Schism, Weber was about

114

the last composer who could turn his hand to anything from symphonies and operas to popular songs and waltzes. Thereafter composers, performers and audiences divided themselves into black and white sheep: the devotees of " serious " or " classical " music and the addicts of " popular " or " light " music. But this is not the place to anticipate what I am going to say later.

It may be argued that Beethoven (1770–1827), like Bach (1685–1750), was in the main a traditionalist. It may be said that Beethoven is distinguished chiefly by reason of his development of the eighteenth-century style; whereas Weber, who was only sixteen years younger, was an innovator. There is a great deal of truth in this. On the other hand, the works of Beethoven which have had the greatest significance for posterity have been those of his later maturity, the big piano sonatas and the four last string quartets. Not that I in any way belittle the symphonies. But' they are all on classical models, developed, it is true, to a perfection of form and content greater than had been achieved before. They were, nevertheless, classical in structure and outlook. With his later works, on the other hand, we see the burgeoning of the Romantic Movement. Particularly is this true of the posthumous quartets. · I do not mean to give the impression that this was a ₅sudden development. The germs of it were latent from the middle period onwards. It is to Beethoven that must be ascribed the dawn of the Romantic Movement with all its fruitful, and in some respects disastrous, consequences.

\*

### (iii) THE GREAT RUSSIANS (1908–c. 1830)

Once more we must rely largely on recorded music to give us an impression of that curious phenomenon, the music of the Great Russian Composers. Curious, because Art-music in Russia erupted as suddenly with Glinka (1803–1857) as did literature with Pushkin (1799–1837). · Were this any more than the briefest outline of musical history, it would be proper to relate all these musical developments which we are discussing to the other artistic, scientific and social events in the world in which ' they took place. As it is, this proper study must be left to some other full-length book, such as the subject deserves.

For practical purposes the last and present representative

of Russian Music is Stravinsky (*b.* 1882), whom we have discussed at some length already.

We must in this Section turn our attention to his immediate predecessors, assuming (as I do with every composer mentioned) that the reader has, through the medium of the gramophone, become familiar with his work so that he can see from what it derived.

We begin, then, with Rimsky-Korsakov (1844–1908). There is here a direct connection between cause and effect: Stravinsky was one of his pupils. His first works are saturated with influences of the master, as may be seen in *Fireworks* (often heard at Promenade Concerts), *The Nightingale* [58] and *The Firebird* [58]. Rimsky-Korsakov had the superb (and justified) effrontery to write a book on orchestration illustrated by examples from his own works. He, in common with most of the Russian composers, was an amateur musician in a very real, and by no means derogatory, sense. He was in the navy. Cui (1835–1918) was in the army. Borodin (1834–1887) was a chemist. Tchaikovsky (1840–1893) and Mussorgsky (1835–1881) must be singled out for special mention; the former for his symphonic and theatre music, the latter particularly for his operas.

Individual though all of the Russian composers are, they have in common a peculiar richness of flavour derived from the native quasi-barbaric music upon which so much of their work was founded. The different provinces of old Russia were found to have an immense store of folk-music which was collected assiduously by its discoverers and made the basis of Art-music. The Russian musical genius has shown itself mostly in the form of operas, ballets and symphonic poems, the stories of which were taken direct from historical events or local legends. All of this music was late in becoming known to the outside world. Its importation into Europe was due to a few ardent enthusiasts in the first decade of this century. The impact of this wild and exciting new music seems to have been terrific, although I am too young to have witnessed it. The music sprang from Russia and has remained Russian. The tunes themselves are vigorous and simple, gaining much of their effect from short phrases reiterated time and time again.

In parenthesis, it may be pointed out that this extreme Russian nationalism has never proved a limitation in the sense that the nationalism of Spanish music has. In precisely the same way all Spanish Art-music is founded upon national traditions. So much have Spanish composers insisted on this narrow nationalism that it would be scarcely too much to say that full appreciation of Spanish music is limited to the Spanish. Naturally everyone can respond to the seduction of the more obvious features, such as the idiosyncratic measure of the national dances like the Tango and the sound of the castanets. But I am sure that no one but a Spaniard knowing the cultural life of his own community can fully understand the implications of Spanish music derived from allusions to the *flamenco* and other national musical features.

Nevertheless, Russian music remains in a sense an isolated phenomenon. Until comparatively recently it cannot be said to have had an influence on the general musical stream comparable to the influence of the novels of, say, Dostoievsky. There is no space to do more than cite examples of recorded music.

Rimsky-Korsakov (1844–1908): Bridal Cortège from *Le Coq d'Or* [72]; Scriabin (1871–1915); *Le Poème d'Extase* [73]; Tchaikovsky (1840–1893): *Casse Noisètte Suite* [40]; Balakirev (1836–1910): *Thamar* [74]; Mussorgsky (1835–1881): Coronation Scene from *Boris Godunov* [75]; Cui (1835–1918): *Kaléidoscope* [76]; Borodin (1834–1887): Polovtsi March from *Prince Igor* [77]; Glinka (1803–1857): Overture to *Russlan and Ludmila* [78].

### (iv) " THE CLASSICS "

#### (a) The French (c. 1860–c. 1650)

We now return to the main development of music in Europe. We broke off our study of the French Romantics with Berlioz (1803–1869).

At this point we are confronted once more by the difficulty of classification. Are the composers whom we are about to consider " Romantic " or " Classical " in their outlook? The most cursory examination shows that the first half-dozen of them do not conveniently fit into either category. But I must insist once more that labels are conveniences. We must remember that it is we who tie on the labels: we must not be tied by them, and commit the mistake of trying to force every composer into this or that category without realising that we place them there purely as a matter of convenience and not from a conviction that they necessarily and truly belong.

117

According to my interpretation, then, the immediate precursors of Berlioz were transitional between the Classical and the Romantic Schools proper. They were traditionalists in so far as they largely accepted many of the Classical conventions, and they broke new ground in so far as they looked forward, unconsciously, if you like, to the Romantics who were to follow them.

In the first place we must mention two foreign invasions which exercised formative influences on the musical destiny of France. One of these invasions came from Germany in the persons of Meyerbeer (1791–1864) and Gluck (1714–1787); the other from Italy, consisting of an influx of Rossini (1792–1868) and Cherubini (1760–1842). It will be seen from a comparison of the dates of these composers that they could not all have come at once. Meyerbeer and Rossini were contemporaries: Cherubini was a generation older; and Gluck nearly a century before them.

In the second place, there were the truly French composers of this period: Halévy (1799–1862), Auber (1782–1871), Boieldieu (1775–1834) and Méhul (1763–1817).

All of these composers, the foreigners who visited or settled in France and the native products, were primarily composers of opera. Of purely instrumental music it seems that there was during this time a partial eclipse.

I will select as representative of this transitional period Hérold's overture to *Zampa* [79], which is unfortunately an old recording. But this, as well as the earliest, period of music is badly served by the gramophone companies.

We turn now to what are perhaps the three greatest names in this period of French musical history: Rameau (1683–1764), Couperin (1668–1733) and Lully (1639–1687).

Rameau (1683–1764) was a prodigy. He early turned his attention to musical theory, and among his most important contributions in this field was his discovery of what are termed the Inversions of Chords. That is to say, he was the first to lay down that the chords E–G–C and G–C–E are really only the First and Second Inversions of the one chord C–E–G, which is its " Root Position."

Ex. 9

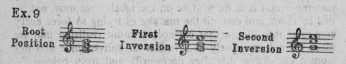

Root Position     First Inversion     Second Inversion

118

This is a thing that every musical child of twelve knows to-day, just as he is conversant with the salient truth of our solarcentric system. Nevertheless, this discovery of Rameau's was of an importance in its own way comparable to Galileo's. In the purely creative sphere Rameau produced much harpsichord music of great charm and considerable importance, although principally he devoted himself to opera and ballet.

The reader is recommended to hear the delightful record of his *Le Tambourin* [80].

Between *c.* 1660 and 1850 there were five generations of musicians in the Couperin family, comparable in this respect to the Bachs, whom we will come across in the next Section (p. 126). François Couperin (1668–1733), called Couperin le Grand, was famous as a composer for the harpsichord. He has the further distinction of being one of the early writers of Programme Music, which often bore the most whimsical titles.

The only recorded music is in the volume of harpsichord music issued by the Couperin Society [81].

The name of Jean-Baptiste Lully (1632–1687) was originally spelt Lülli, the composer being Italian by birth but French by adoption (in romantic and probably discreditable circumstances connected with a fancy of the Duc de Guise) in early boyhood. He was in many ways an adventurer and an unscrupulous scoundrel. But musically he was of the greatest importance, not only to France but to the rest of Europe as well. He is regarded as the founder of French opera; he established the form of the French Overture, a form which immediately popularised itself and endured for generations, and introduced many original ideas which we have no space to deal with here. He died from an abscess in the big toe caused by hitting himself with a baton while conducting his *Te Deum*. The quality of his music, so alive to-day, can be estimated from a single record which contains the Prelude to *Alceste*, the March from *Thésée* and the Notturno from *Le Triomphe de l'Amour* [82].

Let us pause here to consider the main trend of what had been happening to music in France during this long period of roughly two hundred years.

Those composers whom I designated above as the transitionalists between the Classical School and the later Romantics I represented by Hérold's Overture to *Zampa* [79]. In the early, the truly Classical period, one can trace how the first Romantics such as Berlioz (1803–1869) very clearly arose

119

out of the comparative severity of the Classics which already were tempered with the poetic outlook of Couperin (1668–1733), coloured though they were by the second German and Italian invasions. Properly to estimate the position and importance of Lully, the progenitor, we shall have to wait until we see what was happening between the Paris School (which flourished from the twelfth to the fifteenth centuries) and his own period in the latter part of the seventeenth century.

## (b) The German (c. 1790–c. 1740)

Everyone knows the names, and most people are familiar with the music, of the first two of the four composers whom I have selected to represent this present period. For that reason I will not spend much time on them.

To begin with, I should like to draw attention to the similarities to be found between the earlier music of Beethoven (1770–1827), whose period we have just discussed, and the later music of Mozart (1756–1791) and of Haydn (1732–1809). I suggest that this still absolutely " Classical " music reveals in its later manifestations of Beethoven's latter years the unmistakable transition to the " Romantic." One can follow the lessening of the stylised rigidity until a new appearance of spontaneity shows itself, undisguised (if you like) by the same amount, or the same kind, of artifice which is so characteristic of the purely Classical Music.

One other feature deserves mention : the extreme simplicity of the music of Mozart and Haydn. This simplicity is in some ways more apparent than real. But even in the celebrated *Jupiter* Symphony of Mozart there is no complexity of idea or structure comparable to the late Beethoven.

This point needs elaborating somewhat. Let us jump forward a hundred and seventy years to to-day. All the music I cited in the Section on the Contemporary Scene (page 104) is in its various ways complex both in content and, often, in the mode of its expression.* In the few years immediately following the First World War—things happen quickly nowadays—there was a brief return to simplicity following the

---

* This is extremely liable to be misunderstood. I am not impugning any of the composers mentioned of deliberate obscurantism by wrapping up their thoughts in difficult language. It is implicit that one cannot use for one's ideas vehicles which have already done service to an earlier generation; for which reason no one to-day would dream of writing plays in Shakespearean blank verse or of writing a Bach fugue.

turgidities of the first decade of this century and the last decade of the preceding one. This turgidity and complexity may be regarded as a reaction from the lightness and simplicity of the French Romantics, or in part a continuation and apogee of the German Romantics from late Beethoven onwards. Both interpretations are in my view correct.

And now in the German Classics at present under discussion we see once more the recognition of the virtues of simplicity.

(I hope that the reader will bear with me for selecting these terms Complexity and Simplicity. Without devoting to the point considerably more space than is at my disposal, I cannot adequately protect myself from attack. I can but plead that it is, as always, the reader's business to try to understand what I am trying to say, and my business to try to say what I want as clearly and as concisely as possible. If one of us fails in this, you will put the book down in disgust. But if, finally, I say that in this connection I give as examples of Complexity the Schönberg School, the Wagnerians and German Romantics generally; and as examples of Simplicity the French Romantics such as Boieldieu and the German Classics such as Mozart and Haydn, you should at least see what I mean, even if you do not agree with the labels.)

To return to the similarity between Haydn and early Beethoven. Compare these two records: the Finale of Symphony No. 104 in D major by Haydn [83] and the Finale of the First Symphony in C major by Beethoven [84]. But there is one important difference at least: and that is, that the Romantic later Beethoven was implicit in the Classical early Beethoven, whereas there is no trace of it in Haydn— or, for that matter, in Mozart.

The remaining composer of this period is one of Bach's twenty children, Johann Christian (1735–1782), who already heralded this Simplicity, as a reaction from the terrific contrapuntal complexity of the previous generations, of which his father was the incomparable apex.

His Sinfonia in B flat major [85] shows the influence he had on Mozart.

Finally, Christoph Willibald Gluck (1714–1787), whose greatest operas, despite that he was a German, were Italian and French, may be represented by the Dance of the Blessed Spirits from *Orpheus* [86].

One of the most fertilising influences in European music has been Italian Opera, which, throughout its long history, has permeated Germany, France and England in turn. And in every case it has proved a stimulus to the creation of a form of national opera in the countries concerned. The last great figure of the Italians in this sphere was Puccini (1858–1924), a master of stagecraft and a composer of remarkable invention. In this country his opera *La Bohème* [87] is probably the most popular, although his last work, *Turandot* [88], may well be considered of greater importance.

His predecessor, Verdi (1813–1901), was not exclusively a composer of opera as was Puccini. His *Requiem* [89] is in every way as notable as the operas by which he is best known, *Aida* and *Rigoletto* [90]. It may be mentioned that he exercised considerable influence in France.

Donizetti (1797–1848) and Rossini (1792–1868) were also instrumental in fertilising French opera. In the French music of the period can be clearly seen how the music of these two Italians, who spent so much time in France, influenced the course of events. The light sparkle and vivacity, the use of dramatic musical moments when an abrupt and wholly unexpected chord interrupts the trickling flow of melody, are features borrowed from the Italians.

The first name in this period of the development of Italian Opera is Piccinni (1728–1800). Around him and the German Gluck (1714–1787) arose one of those storms of partisanship which are such diverting features of musical history. Those, one says to oneself, were the days when people really cared for music. Those were the days when rival factions, each acclaiming that his favourite composer was the only one of any importance and the other a second-rate hack, demonstrated in theatres, cafés and streets, and even went to the length of free fights. In our times there have been disturbances at concerts and theatres by members of the audience who did not care for what they were listening to: the first performance of Webern's String Trio at the International Festival of Contemporary Music in Siena (1928) and of Stravinsky's *Rite of Spring* [23] in Paris in 1913 were nearly wrecked by the " antis." I may even be permitted to add that the police had to be sent for during a concert of my own works in London in 1927. But there has been no rivalry between composers comparable to the Gluck-Piccinni feud. In so far as such enthusiastic feelings are indices of intensity of emotion and enjoyment, this lack of partisanship is to be deplored.

It will be seen, or rather heard, from the examples cited above that operatic music has tended to become ever more elaborately anecdotal and illustrative, in conformity with the development of Programme Music. Richness of effect and of effects has in nearly every case been the ultimate achievements of contemporary opera. Exceptions are to be found in deliberate returns to the older æsthetic idea of formalisation as in much of Hindemith's operatic music and in Stravinsky's *Œdipus Rex,* for example. But in the main it is true to say that no action on the stage can pass unnoticed by the music: in the orchestra clocks strike, bells ring and doors open and close with the most ingenious onomatopœic noises. So we can trace this development from Piccinni, whose music was still cast into formal movements the sequences of which were dictated by an elaborate operatic convention, which laid down that after a chorus a solo recitative must come, and this in turn must be followed by an aria. And so on. But even in Piccinni the germs of musical dramatisation are already well developed. They needed but to be elaborated to reach their full efflorescence with Puccini.

Here, for the moment, we will leave Italian opera as such and pass to consideration of things in other countries.

## (vi) THE ENGLISH SCHOOL (1943–*c.* 1100)

It is no concern of mine to push home products. That task can quite comfortably be left to others. We can glance at contemporary activity in this country, and pass on. It does not appear that there is to-day in England any music of significance as far as the big issues and long historical view of the art as a whole are concerned. English Music remains parochial, despite the irresistible infiltration of Continental influences. In a country where peasant costumes and traditions are long since dead, and folk-music is kept precariously alive in the hothouses of the English Folk Dance Society, it cannot be expected that a national tradition on these lines should continue to exist as a vital thing. Ironically enough, insular England was, if only by reason of its Empire and overseas connections generally, the first nation whose people became Citizens of the World. The manifest reluctance of many people to accept this plain fact has resulted in disastrous consequences in almost every sphere. Musically speaking, this resistance has resulted in a great deal of the parochialism mentioned above as well as ill-digested accretions from foreign sources. Music, I maintain, is as international as Science. And no one, surely, is so misguided as to suppose that some particular virtue resides in British Science as such, despite the fact that Science has in this country an unbroken heritage of generations of scientific thought when Englishmen have been among the leaders of the world. This has not been the case with Music, which suffered a sorry eclipse for the better part of a hundred years.

The spectacular expansion of British imperialist-capitalism in the latter half of the nineteenth century imbued many artists of the day with the most romantic notions of the civilising mission of our Island Race. There was a new kind of crusade, aptly expressed in Kipling's slogan, "The White Man's Burden." The spirit of this and the chauvinistic poems of Sir Henry Newbolt provided incentives for heroic musical sagas such as Sir Charles Stanford's *Songs of the Fleet*. This, Sir Hubert Parry's *Jerusalem,* and similar works were performed on weekdays, nicely balanced by pious exercises to suit the requirements of the one-day-a-week religion of the well-to-do. In this latter connection the first and last verses (there are seven in all) of Hymn 584 from *Hymns Ancient & Modern,* Standard Edition, 1869, are worth quoting as an indication of the degradation and cynicism of the official religion of the period, which lent itself with every appearance of willingness to the task of perpetuating the social conditions on which our imperial prosperity was founded. The dynamic markings ("expression marks") should be noticed:

*For a Service for Working Men—Hymn* 584

    *mf* Sons of Labour, dear to Jesus,
           To your homes and work again;
  *cresc.* Go with brave hearts back to duty,
    *dim.* Face the peril, bear the pain;
      *p* Be your dwellings ne'er so lowly,
  *cresc.* Yet remember by your bed
    *mf* That the SON of GOD most holy
    *dim.* Had not where to lay His head.

*mf* Sons of Labour, live for JESUS,
    Be your work your worship too;
In His Name, and to His Glory,
    Do whate'er you find to do,
Till this night of sin and sorrow
    Be for ever overpast,
  *f* And we see the golden morrow,
    Home with JESUS, home at last!

This was the emotional and intellectual colouring of the period. It is only just to say that the music is entirely lacking in distinction.

Nevertheless, the resuscitation of music in this country, though not comparable with the efflorescence produced by the Elizabethan merchant-adventurers, was begun by Sir Hubert Parry (1848–1918) and made a reality by Sir Edward Elgar (1857–1935). Important though the effects of this revival have been for this country, no composer of international consequence has as yet been thrown up.

Vaughan Williams (*b.* 1872), Arnold Bax (*b.* 1883), E. J. Moeran (*b.* 1894), and John Ireland (*b.* 1879) are, nevertheless, notable figures in English music [91]. And, of the younger generation, William Walton (*b.* 1902), Constant Lambert (*b.* 1905) and Benjamin Britten (*b.* 1912) have achieved considerable reputations which extend to every country where contemporary music is played [92].

Our last composer may be said to be Dr. Arne (1710–1778). In the interim England was inundated by a flood of Händelian and Italian Opera, whose tide the national produce was not sufficiently vigorous to withstand. The operas of Arne number over thirty. The songs, " Blow, blow, thou winter wind " and " Under the greenwood tree " from *As You Like It* [93] are worth hearing.

Prior to Arne was a number of great figures, among them Dr. Blow (1648–1708) and Henry Purcell (1658–1695). The music of Blow is unfortunately not readily accessible. He was a voluminous composer of anthems, songs and harpsichord music.

Henry Purcell (1658–1695) was in every way a more important figure. He is generally regarded as the flower of English composers, although until lately his works have been strangely neglected. A Purcell Society has been formed, however, and now many of his most important works are available on the gramophone, among them his celebrated opera *Dido and Æneas* [94]. But his *Rejoice in the Lord Alway* [95], from the Columbia History of Music, should also be heard.

The sixteenth and seventeenth centuries constitute the real period of English music. From the large number of composers whose work has come down to us I have room here to mention only a few outstanding names, such as Orlando Gibbons [44] (1583–1625), Thomas Weelkes [44] (157?–1623), John Dowland [96] (1563–1626), John Bull (*c.* 1562–1628), Thomas Morley [44] (1558–1603), William Byrd (1538–1623) and Thomas Tallis (152?–1585). All of these were composers of madrigals and writers for the lute. Musically, as in many other ways, it was indeed a Golden Age for England, when her composers were known and famed all over Europe.

We must leave this subject asking questions about anonymous composers, many of whose works even have been lost and forgotten. John Dunstable (*d.* 1453) appears as a shadowy figure. References to him are to be found in French writings of the period. All that is certain is that by inference there must have been a flourishing and important school of English composers long before this time. Reference has already been made to the monk John Fornsete (*fl.* 1226), who is supposed to have been the composer of *Summer is Icumen In* [14]. It is impossible to suppose that a work of such complexity should suddenly have emerged without native ancestors. Also the name of John Odington, who is known to have flourished in 1280 and to have died in 1316, is unmistakably English; although it is known that he lived most of his life in France, where records show him to have been famed as a great English composer.

It is always possible that further research will in time bring these early stars in our musical firmament to light once more. Certainly the music of these early times which has survived destruction in wars and revolutions, the Dissolution of the Monasteries and later enthusiasms of the Puritans, is sufficiently alive to-day to make such researches valuable for posterity.

### (vii) THE EARLY GERMANS (1750–*c.* 1650)

And now we go back to Germany, which took up so much time and space a little while ago.

We start with the father of the two Bachs, Johann Christian (1735–1782) and Carl Philipp Emanuel (1714–1788), whom we mentioned then. Johann Sebastian Bach (1685–1750) was the apex of a long line of contrapuntal writers. Already in his time he was something of an old fogey, doing little that was new—apart from popularising the new tuning of the scale, the Mean Temperament, which had such far-reaching consequences—but doing what he did so much better than anyone else that perfection is no extreme word to apply to his music. Readers will be familiar with the kind of music he wrote, and the Fugue analysed on page 35 will be sufficient guide.

Of a very different stamp and calibre was his contemporary, George Frederick Händel (1685–1759), who was in part responsible for swamping the dying music native to England with his ponderous bulk and vast output. It is said that the only original tune Händel wrote is that known as *The Harmonious Blacksmith*. However untrue that may be literally, I have it on the authority of the late Dr. Charles Wood that there may be seen in the Fitzwilliam Museum at Cambridge some of the composer's notebooks wherein he had jotted down tunes which he had heard and liked, many of them with a mark against them to indicate that he had himself used them later. This accusation of plagiarism used by his enemies can be made to suit other great composers equally. Bach used dozens of tunes by Luther as well as traditional German tunes; and so, indeed, did every great composer when it suited his purpose. The charge is a foolish one, and should never have been made. There is a nobility and sweep in his music, and a fine dramatic intensity in his operas. For an example of his music that is not too hackneyed, listen to the Harpsichord Concerto in B flat [97] and " The Lord is a Man of War " [98] from *Israel in Egypt*, and compare them with the music of Bach. There is a striking contrast. Bach, the paid servant of pettifogging provincial princelings and churchmen, producer of music whose poignancy is unmatched; Händel, recking little of where the next penny was coming from, intent, one might say, only on satisfying the wider needs of the English public for good, solid, straightforward music, which to-day still has its appreciative audience among the mass of the people.

The immediate predecessors of Bach and Händel were Fux (1660–1750) and Buxtehude [99] (1637–1707). It was the latter who was the organist so much admired by Bach when he was a young man. Unfortunately the music of neither is readily accessible to-day. It must suffice to indicate that they were in the main stream of development of which Bach was the culminating point.

With the three names of Scheidt [100] (1587–1654), Schein [101] (1586–1630) and Schütz [102] (1585–1672) we come near the beginnings of German Art-music, which was fertilised by contact with Italy (see folding chart).

There is no space here to go into the earliest known period, of which the music is familiar, generally speaking, only to scholars.

And so we leave the German-speaking countries, from which so much music has come. We are getting near the end of this very brief sketch of the Genesis of Music in Europe.

### (viii) THE EARLY ITALIANS (1750–c. 1550)

Properly speaking, this Section falls under two distinct heads. But for convenience we will group the two periods together. The first of these periods is really concerned with the Classical Italians from Martini (1706–1784) to Corelli (1659–1719). The style of the music has something of early Mozart in it. Indeed, Mozart, born fifty years later, was influenced by the Italians of his day to a considerable extent.

We will take as a sample piece of the period a Sonata by Domenico Scarlatti (1685–1725) [103]. It is interesting to note, by the way, the amazing difference in style between this Sonata and the music of Bach, who was born in the same year. Music in the Italy of this time had emancipated itself from the formal counterpoint which was still being written in Germany.

The second period, the true " Early Italians," ends with Cavalli (1600–1676) and Peri (1561–1633), already mentioned in connection with the first known operas, and goes back to the elder Gabrieli (1510–1586).

Two big names come in between: Monteverde (1567–1643) and Palestrina (1525–1594). The former also wrote operas of great beauty, such as *Orfeo* [22] and *La Coronazione di Poppœa* [104]. The latter was the apex of the Italian contrapuntists, just as Bach was in his day. We need not worry here about what came before him. Here we see the pure sixteenth-century style in all its complexity and stylistic perfection.

Finally we note that the elder Gabrieli [105] (1510–1586) was a pupil of Adrian Willaert (1480–1562), the Flemish founder of the Venetian School. Thus is the torch of learning handed from country to country.

### (ix) THE EARLY FRENCH (1700–c. 1550)

In France during the sixteenth and seventeenth centuries— prior, that is, to Lully (1632–1687), who was the last French composer we dealt with, and after the early Paris School, with which music in Europe starts—music is distinguished chiefly for the work of the lutenists and early harpsichordists. These latter date from Henry Nivers (c. 1617–post 1701) to de Chambonnières (1602–c. 1672); the lutenists from Mésangeau, who was born some time before 1600 and died in 1639, to Claude Gervaise (fl. 1550).

In this period there still survived what I surmise to have been the oriental influence of music with a more or less fixed accompaniment played by the singer himself with the vocal part so free as to have something of the manner of improvisation, just as Arab music to-day has. It is important in this respect to realise that European Art-music had its roots in the ancient Hebrew sacred music, which spread around both shores of the Mediterranean; north through Greece and Rome, whence the Church carried the traditions all over Europe; south along the coast to Spain, where the two streams met in confluence. You will hear on a record cited in the final Section (page 130) of this history a song by Maître Léonin, organist of Notre Dame in Paris in about 1100, which is remarkably like music sung by the cantors in synagogues to this day.

To go back a moment to the early clavecinists,* Louis Couperin (1626–1661) wrote music which in its freedom from restrictions and indulgence in fantasy is extraordinarily like that of the English Purcell, who lived a generation later. And so we get a perfect sequence of development back to the grace of de Chambonnières (1602–c. 1672), the founder of the French School of Clavecinists; the sonorous gravity of Pinel (fl. 1640); the experiments in freedom of Mésangeau (ante 1600–1639); the florid counterpoint of Guédron (1565–

---

* The Clavecin (French for Harpsichord) was a keyboard instrument whose strings were plucked by quills; whereas the strings of the later pianoforte are hit by hammers.

*post* 1620); and the formalised severity of du Caudray (1549–1609) and Gervaise (*fl.* 1550).    Two further characteristics of these early composers may be mentioned: the free adaptations of secular tunes to sacred uses, and the broken rhythms of the dance measures, which often have only one strain of 5 bars—6 bars—3 bars, making 14 in all.

## (x) THE NETHERLANDS POLYPHONIC SCHOOL (1620–*c.* 1420)

The last representative of this great school of composers, Sweelinck (1562–1621), provides a link with the early French lutenists whom we have just been discussing.  Similarly Adrian Willaert (1480–1562) was the bridge, as it were, which carried the traditions of the Netherlands Polyphony to Italy, as mentioned above (page 128).  Josquin des Prés (1445–1521), the theoretician, Johannes Tinctoris (1446–1511) and Dufay (*ante* 1400–1474), and Binchois (*c.* 1400–1460), the father of them all, are some of the more important figures.  The record of *Christe Redemptor* and *Conditor alme siderum* [106] by Dufay appears to be the only music of this period available on the gramophone, apart from some anonymous works.

All of this early music is difficult to examine in detail. Most of it is in manuscript, and then in a notation which only scholars (of whom I am not one) can read.  The best one can do is to take the few examples there are and quote them as indicative of the loveliness that is inherent in music. The cursory manner in which I have seemingly dismissed the early Italians (page 128) and the Early French (page 129) is not due to any desire to create an adverse balance of importance.  On the contrary, if I may openly avow my own predilections for a moment now that we are at the end of this little outline of history, the music of these early times makes more appeal to me than that of other periods on which I have here expended more space.

## (xi) THE PARIS SCHOOL (*c.* 1370–*c.* 1100)

And so we come to the end, or, rather, the beginnings, of Art-music in Europe.

Some anonymous works [1 and 2] and two lovely songs [107], by Pérotin (*c.* 1120–*c.* 1170) and Léonin (*fl.* 1100) must suffice for the earliest known Art-music.  These two composers were both organists at Notre Dame in Paris.  The anonymous works may be from the Flemish School or not. I don't know.  Anyway, they are fairly representative of the pure monodic style, singular in the depth of emotion and religious fervour which has in Europe been the source of the best of her art in certain periods.

For it is a fact that the official Church has not been consistent in its attitude to the secular and pagan activities of the people. There have been times when popular traditions have been so strong that the only course open to the Church was to permit indulgence of traditional rites, even within the church buildings themselves. The festival of Christmas is in fact the ancient Mithraic ritual of sun-worship. And orgiastic celebrations of fertility-rites have been common enough; although to-day all that survives is the rather tame Harvest Festival, with its decorations of sheaves of corn and prize leeks from the squire's garden.

On all these occasions, purely secular music, often with licentious songs, have been permitted in church. Even at the time of the most highly stylised Church-music the basic material of the sung masses was frequently taken from secular songs. When the Lutheran Reformation allowed the congregation to sing, instead of compelling them to be passive spectators of an elaborate ritual in an alien tongue which none could understand, it was necessary to go to the people for music that they could easily learn. Luther therefore did the obvious thing, and used traditional secular tunes which the congregation already knew. Thus the style and content of music is always conditioned by the form of society in which it is produced.

The reflection is here induced that Art is essentially timeless. One talks of the " development " of this or that period of an art as if the products of any one time were " better " or more advanced than those of any other. This, I maintain, is violently untrue. Music was already before this time (the fifteenth century) perfect of its kind and in its way. To say that Schönberg or Wagner or Beethoven or Mozart were in any sense " better," more elaborate, more highly developed, than Bach or Scarlatti or Palestrina or Dufay is nonsense. The music of all is different. The aims and intentions of the composers were different; their technical equipment was different; they lived in different worlds, with different intellectual, social and historical backgrounds. Consequently, as I see it, it was impossible for people to write contrapuntal music in a world where men believed the earth to be flat and the universe terracentric. It was Galileo who, primarily, made possible the invention of the projection of perspectives on to a plane and, similarly, of counterpoint in music.

All these things need working out and relating to each other. To do so would occupy many years of research and a whole book devoted to the subject. I mention the above instance as an example of the lines on which I am thinking in my interpretation of the History of Music.

And at that I must leave it.


# VIII

## SERIOUS MUSIC AND POPULAR MUSIC: THE GREAT SCHISM

THE Great Schism was the title of an article by Mr. Edwin Evans in *The Music Lover,* a now defunct weekly paper of which he was Editor. In it he pointed out the calamity which overtook music when the distinction between " serious " or " classical " * music and " popular " music became a reality. It was, he said, a disaster as serious as the Great Schism which overtook religion in an earlier time.

It must not be thought that this differentiation between so-called serious and popular music has always existed. The schism dates from the introduction of the Waltz.

Before we go any farther I want to distinguish between Popular Music and Folk-music. Folk-music has always been a fertile spring, a spontaneous expression of mostly anonymous composers. It is music which comes from the people. The English folk-tunes such as *Gathering Peas-cods* and the Austrian Ländler are examples of folk-music. Popular Music, on the other hand, is music written *for* the people. Of such is the dance-music of our own day. The study of popular music would be an important adjunct to sociology. In it one could trace the romanticised love-theme of Victorian times, with frequent death by misadventure of a little girl or her daddy, passing through the early days of jazz of the Let's-Get-Together Everybody's-Doing-It type to the nostalgic phase when Lew Kern and Ike Zizzbaum put their heads together

* Note that the word " classical " is used here and in what follows in a totally different sense from the opposition to " romantic " previously defined. It is clear that Mr. Edwin Evans means by " classical music " what I have throughout this book called Art-music.

to produce a poem the burthen of which was that the singer wished to be back on the old farm, frequently situated in Kentucky. The joint authors then handed their effusion to Alf Lohr, who in his turn collaborated with Mo Isaacs, Duke Smith and even Ron Rogers to concoct a tune.* It is these talented gentlemen who produce for mass consumption the Popular Music of to-day. Of true Folk-music there is to-day very little evidence. The National Anthem of Republican Spain might be cited as a recent example; and so, too, the American Negro "Spirituals." But in the main people of to-day seem to prefer to be passive consumers rather than active producers of music.

Let me quote from Mr. Evans's article mentioned above: "The greatest misfortune that has ever befallen the art of music is the schism that has divided it into two worlds, those of so-called 'classical' and 'popular' music. It is as great a misfortune as that which overtook religion in the Great Schism which rent the civilised world of its day in twain. But, somebody will timidly ask, has this distinction not always existed under one name or another? The answer is most emphatically no. For centuries the only recognised distinction that may be said to correspond with it was that between sacred and profane music. Men made music for the glory of God or the entertainment of their fellow-men, but in either case they made it with all the skill that was available in their day—and, what is more important, it was the same skilled musicians who made it.

"The great Bach family comprised in its earlier generations not only organists and cantors, but also town-pipers—we should call them conductors of municipal orchestras—who played for the entertainment of the public. Bach himself, though he wrote Church Cantatas with what some listeners-in nowadays consider to have been exaggerated zeal, also wrote music which, believe it or not, was found entertaining in its day. Haydn was a popular idol. Mozart would write for a Court Ball as readily as for High Mass. Schubert, in writing his immortal Lieder, had no other thought—but only another standard—than that of writing drawing-room songs. Weber composed the *Favourite Waltzes* of the Empress Marie Louise for the occasion of her Majesty's visit to Strassburg in 1810. It is true that she had never heard them before her arrival there, but Weber did not think it a

* These names are fictitious.

133

grave risk to take, for she was Viennese, and therefore had such excellent musical taste that his waltzes were certain to find favour, not because he was 'classical,' but because he was a skilled musician who should know how to write good waltzes.

"Thereupon a change comes over the scene. Under the influence of the Romantic Movement musicians began to put their art upon a pedestal of idealism—which was good— and keep her there as securely as in a nunnery, or as the statue of Liberty with her back to New York—which was bad. Schubert might have been in his way a waltz-king, but after him the line divides. In the kingdom of the dance the crown passed to Lanner, Keler Bela and three generations of the Strauss dynasty, whilst in the temple of idealism it passed to Mendelssohn, Schumann and Brahms. Thenceforth serious musicians would not demean themselves by 'ear-tickling,' any more than waltz-kings would try to write symphonies. On either side it would have been incongruous for them to do so, though Mozart did both cheerfully without thinking any the less of himself. Why should he?

"As the nineteenth century grew older the schism grew wider . . . and has widened ever since until composers, performers, and most of all listeners, seem to think of themselves as belonging to two different worlds. Worse still: each of these two worlds has developed its own particular brand of snobbishness, for it is just as snobbish to deride a man for being an alleged high-brow as it is to patronise him as a groundling for liking a tune he can whistle. . . . It was reserved for our democratic age to bring forward people who will say, not regretfully, but boastfully, that the best is not for the likes of them. Would it not show a better self-esteem if they boldly declared that the best music of any kind, whether symphony or jazz, was just barely good enough for them—and live up to it?"

This excellent article from which I have quoted so freely is in my opinion numbered among the most significant that Edwin Evans ever wrote. He exposes the whole tragic situation. What has to be done is to find a way out of this *impasse*.

I tried to show in the introductory remarks to the last Section (page 98) that the threefold cleavage between Art-music, Folk-music and Commercialised Jazz to-day is a necessary consequence of the class-divisions of society. I have tried to indicate here and there, that at all times in history every social class has produced its own music. If this view is correct, it follows that complete unity in music cannot be achieved until society develops into a classless community.

That is not to say that nothing can be done *now*. I believe it to be the duty of every composer to ally himself with the progressive sections of the people, and to attempt to write music which, without entailing the composer being "untrue to himself," will assist in forwarding the aspirations and well-being of mankind.

Mr. Evans, in the article quoted above, takes the advent of the Waltz as the significant moment in the Great Schism. Why is this? The Waltz was music appropriated from the people (Austrian Ländler) by the ruling class at the time of the Congress of Vienna; and this coincided with the industrial revolution and the rise of the bourgeois-capitalist class. Since then, as Mr. Evans points out, the gulf has widened in accordance with the greater divisions within society itself.

It is up to us to close this breach. We can then envisage a future when music will no longer be the prerogative of the few, but will be the heritage of all.

## IX

## INTERPRETATION AND PERFORMANCE

IN the Section on Notation (page 39) I pointed out how very inadequate are our musical symbols, despite their complexity. Since the dawn of Romanticism in music began with Beethoven composers have in general been ever more meticulous in getting as close as they can to an exact expression of their intentions. In other words, composers have relied less and less on Interpretation in an endeavour to ensure a Performance of their music. Every slightest ornament is written out in full where before various squiggly signs known as Mordants written over the notes were deemed sufficient. Even these were not always written in the music. It was left to the skill and musicianship of the performer to put in these ornaments where he thought best. More curious still was a species of musical shorthand known as Figured Bass. This left practically everything to the imagination of the interpreter of the music. All the composer did was to write in the bass part (usually in accompaniments to songs). Under every note he wrote one or two numerals. These numerals indicated the Intervals of the important notes above the written bass-notes. The figures $\frac{5}{3}$, for example, denote the root position of the common chord, the 3 indicating the third, the 5 indicating the dominant, above the written note. Similarly the figure 6 denotes the first inversion. Where E is the note given, the sixth above, C, is the operative note, the intermediate G completing the chord being implicit. (See also Ex. 9, page 118.) From this skeleton the interpreter was expected to be able to reconstruct the composer's idea, or an approximation sufficiently close to it as not to matter. This was a fairly simple business when the vocabulary of music was small. Even so, there was ample scope for outrageously false interpretations. It might be that all the composer wrote was

Ex. 10

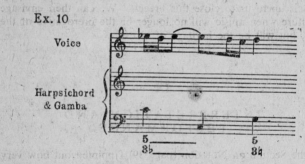

By this the interpreter understood

Ex. 11

But it might well be that the musical context might demand an elaboration of this basic statement into

Ex. 12

Voice

Harpsichord
& Gamba

But when the harmonic vocabulary of music became enlarged it was increasingly difficult and finally impossible to
employ this shorthand. In addition the composer had become fully self-conscious. The individual in art was exalted.
No longer did any art deal in the abstractions of natural
expression. All the arts became highly individual. The
ancient classical attitude of statements of fundamentals had
gone. The psychological aspect was stressed. A parallel can
be seen in literature and in painting. The qualities of uni-
versality which make the dramas of Sophocles supreme were
no longer possible for a romantic such as Shakespeare, who
dealt exclusively in personalities. Characters on the stage
and in literature became "types." The world is invited to
take an interest in their personal problems, displayed by a
genius like Shakespeare in such a masterly way that it is
possible for one to recognise one's friends in the skilfully
drawn "characters."

Similarly in music it was no longer possible for a composer
to remain anonymous, as the majority of early composers was
perfectly content to be. For the most part it is rare to find
a composer of any time up to the sixteenth century attaching
his signature to his work with a flourish, proclaiming thereby
that it is his work and no other's. We know to-day that so-
and-so was the composer of this or that piece of music from
other evidence. This was all changed by the advent of
"the personal note," an illuminating expression (of which
the Oxford English Dictionary surprisingly takes no account)
whose significance in this connection was pointed out by that

great doctor and writer on art, Georg Groddeck.

There is, however, another aspect of Interpretation. This is concerned with the *kind* of music, some music by its very nature requiring more " interpretation " than other. Of such is the music of Chopin, for example. Every amateur pianist knows that it is impossible to " perform " Chopin. The nature of the musical thought is such that, no matter how many verbal directions may supplement the written notes, it makes nonsense of the music to play it as if the truth, the whole truth and nothing but the truth reside in them. All kinds of nuances and inflections, variations of tempo and dynamics, are essential to the music. The bare notes scarcely make sense of themselves unless the player is able by some mental alchemy to get behind the crotchets and quavers at the essence of the composer's intentions and distil from these obscure shadows what he can.

And here we come up against a difficulty. If so much depends on the player, whom are we to trust? Clearly the " rightness " of an interpretation must vary with the interpreter; and interpretative artists are much like other people in their reluctance to modify an attitude once they have declared it. They nail the colours of virtuosity to the mast of independence and won't haul them down for anybody. Thus, failing the higher authority of the composer himself, in the end we can but rely on our own feelings, and if driven beyond all bearing by the divergencies between our own ideas and the ones put before us, our sorry best, more often than not, is to call the man a fool and go our ways.

The odd thing is that when this process of " interpretation " is applied extensively to, say, Händel, the results are so devastating as to drive any sensitive soul out of the room.

Do not immediately run away with the idea that I am saying that Händel was able to write down precisely what he wanted. But the nature of his musical thought was such that he was able to approximate more closely to his intentions than the frequently nebulous music of romantics such as Chopin, cited above, or Debussy. A certain amount of imagination, that is, interpretation, is essential, no matter what the music may be. Which is why performers and interpreters are both right. In short, it is a matter of degree, not of kind, and varies with the laziness or inability of the composer to make himself clear, different kinds of music

138

needing more or less explication as the case may be. For I must take it that every composer wishes his music to be Performed and not Interpreted, to have the actuality of his own intentions realised rather than some spurious invention of whoever's hands his work may fall into.

Therefore in some respects the person I would lay by the heels is the composer, rather than his complementary adjunct the pianist, conductor or whatever he may be. The composer can never explain himself enough. And the trouble often is not that he cannot, but that he does not even try. When Shaw complained that Ibsen's plays were unintelligible unless they were produced on the stage by a man of genius, Ibsen's reply was: "What I have said, I have said." To which Shaw very properly retorted: "Precisely. But what you haven't said, you haven't said."

The justness of an interpretation or performance must therefore be left to the consensus of opinion.

## X

## EMPHASIS ON THE PERFORMER

It strikes me from time to time how odd it is that the public sets such store by the Performer. In a world such as ours to-day, where success and importance are measured in terms of money, one naturally looks to the film "stars" for the most striking figures. The income for 1937 (the latest figures available at the time of writing) of Mr. Fredric March, an American film actor, was £96,937. This is an index of the phenomenon, so curious to me, that people will go to see a film because this or that actor appears in it, irrespective of what the film may be about—if it is about anything.

The same phenomenon is observable on the stage and in the concert world. In neither of these professions does the popularity, and therefore the monetary income, of artists reach such astronomical figures. A musical conductor (as official documents describe the profession, presumably to avoid confusion with other denominations such as tram and omnibus conductors) is ordinarily not comparable. There is a certain coyness about musicians generally regarding these matters, in strong contrast to what some might consider the blatancy of certain film stars. So that in such case where I might be in a position to give comparative figure with a fair degree of accuracy, a reticence which I mus respect prevents me from doing so. Suffice it that a con ductor is fortunate if he makes one-twentieth as much a Mr. Fredric March, although a popular singer can earn pos sibly one-tenth.

The composer of concert-music is lucky if he gets int three figures. And then it is a considerable exception. Mos composers do not earn their livelihoods from their work They are able to compose music only if they have a mor or less assured income from other sources. But a compose of " popular " tunes such as Irving Berlin may have royaltie from a single song amounting to £5,000.

It is all a question of supply and demand. Personalitie are what people want; and they are willing to pay for thei wants. It is I, and a few other eccentrics, who are peculiar. I and my kind would not walk across the street, as the saying is, to hear the most famous violinist or pianist in the world unless he was performing music that we wanted to hear.

It is this emphasis on the performer that once more takes us back to the beginnings of the Romantic Movement. I will conclude this brief sketch with the entertaining story of the famous singer Farinelli, who was born in 1705 at Naples and died in 1782.

It was the custom in those days for boys with promising voices to be castrated to preserve the treble voice. Apocryphal stories are told that while a boy Farinelli had an accident while riding. But there is little doubt that the operation was deliberately performed, with the result that he retained what is commonly said to have been the most perfect soprano voice ever heard. He visited England in 1734 when Händel was busy producing his operas here. Farinelli sang at the Theatre in Lincoln's Inn in an opera *Arteserse,* with music mostly by Farinelli's brother, Broschi. It is said that the first note of the air " Son qual nave " in this opera was begun by Farinelli with such delicacy, swelled very gradually to such an amazing volume and then subsided once more to the delicate *pianissimo* with which he began, that the audience applauded him for five minutes. His rapidity of execution after this opening note was such that the orchestra was unable to keep up with him. On another occasion Farinelli was inging the part of a hero bound in chains. His cruel tormentor, a part taken by Senesino, was overcome by the touching beauty of Farinelli's voice; and, forgetting the part he had to play, rushed across the stage and embraced Farinelli in tears. The Prince of Wales presented him with a gold snuff-box, a pair of diamond knee-buckles, and a purse of a hundred guineas. During the four years he spent in London his salary was never less than £5,000 a year—a very considerable sum in those days. He returned to Italy, where he built himself a magnificent house out of the savings from his sojourn in England, calling it *English Folly*. He is credited with having alleviated the depressive mania of King Philip V of Spain by singing to him. The monarch had long abandoned interest in the outside world. But, having heard Farinelli once, he allowed himself to be shaved for the first time for many weeks, and thereafter retained Farinelli at his court at a salary of 50,000 francs, commanding him to sing the same four songs every night. This he did for nearly three years, without any variation, and was thus lost to the world of music. Philip appointed him Prime Minister, which post he held until the king's death in 1746.

It will be clear from all this that interpretative artists commonly have little or nothing to do with art. They are exhibitionists pure and simple, as much as those queer ladies and unfrocked clergy who exhibit themselves in barrels at seaside resorts. Music for them is a vehicle for their own personal advancement. And a highly profitable one, too.

It is clear, then, that the majority of audiences go to public performances mainly to hear this or that famous artist. Kreisler, Gigli, Toscanini, will always fill a concert-hall, no matter what music they perform. The last-named is certainly an artist in the truest sense of the word. It so happens that he is also a superb showman, which attribute is surely an indispensable part of the artist's equipment. But too often showmanship is made use of to display a well-formed larynx; and not many people mind that there is no real musical sense or sensibility there. Certainly people are entitled to their enjoyment of these physical feats. But it has nothing to do with music, which is debased into a vehicle for personal display and advancement.

# XI

# ACTIVE LISTENING

ALREADY in the last Section (page 139) mention had to be made of the audience in relation to music. I now want to consider the listener exclusively.

What does the listener want from music? I have already pointed out that for the majority of concert-goers the appeal of what is called in advertisements for concerts "personal appearances" of people famous for their physical prowess in brilliance of execution of showy pieces fulfils all their needs. Signor X appears at the Royal Albert Hall in London with a programme of half a dozen songs which serve to arouse the audience's impatient enthusiasm, and then the real business of the evening begins with the Encores, which take the form of old favourites which everyone knows. Signor X makes a lot of money, so does his manager, so does his agent. His audience are enraptured and grateful to the celebrity for being so good as to sing eight or nine songs over and above the advertised programme. In short, a good time is had by all. I am not so unkind as to wish to deprive these good people of their simple pleasures, or even to tell them that they ought not to enjoy them. I do not set myself up to be anybody's judge in these things. All I do is to protest that it is not music.

I repeat the question. What does the listener want from music? One answer is provided by the request with which every amateur performer is familiar: "Play us something we know." This is an interesting requirement. It shows that, as someone has previously said, popularity is synonymous with familiarity. To listen to unknown music demands a mental effort from which the generality of people in our society is averse.

The reason for this, I believe, is inherent in our social system. Only very few people have the privilege of an education that trains or even encourages them to think. This has always been the case since the beginnings of class-society.

The student of history will remember that the extensive introduction of machinery about a hundred and fifty years ago faced the ruling class with the necessity of teaching the workers how to use it; that is, of teaching them to read, write and cipher. The further consequence that this knowledge would also lay open the workers to the influence of " dangerous thoughts " was, however, perceived by many at the time. The ruling class was therefore in a dilemma, which is well expressed by two quotations. In 1807 a Mr. Giddy rose in the House of Commons and delivered himself as follows:

" However specious in theory the project might be, of giving education to the labouring masses of the poor, it would in effect be found to be prejudicial to their morals and happiness; it would teach them to despise their lot in life, instead of making them good servants in agriculture and other laborious employments to which their rank in society has destined them, instead of teaching them subordination, it would render them factious and refractory, as was evident in the manufacturing counties; it would enable them to read seditious pamphlets, vicious books, and publications against Christianity; it would render them insolent to their superiors; and in a few years the results would be that the legislature would find it necessary to direct the strong arm of power towards them, and to furnish the executive magistrate with much more vigorous laws than were now in force."

*(Hansard, quoted in Hammond's " Town Labourer.")*

This weighty argument so frightened the Government that the proposal to educate " the labouring masses of the poor " was dropped. However, the matter was reopened in 1839, when it was pointed out in a semi-official report to Parliament that the dangers of ignorance were, if anything, greater than the dangers of at least some knowledge. This report, after drawing attention to the probability that " persons and property will, in certain parts of the country, be so exposed to violence as materially to affect the prosperity of our manufactures and commerce, to shake the mutual confidence of mercantile men, and to diminish the stability of our political and social institutions " drew the following conclusion:

" It is astonishing to us that the party calling themselves Conservatives should not lead the van in promoting the security of property and the maintenance of public order. To restore the working classes to their former state of incurious and contented apathy is impossible, if it were desirable. If they are to have knowledge, surely it is part of a wise and virtuous Government to do all in its power to secure to them useful knowledge and to guard them against pernicious opinions."

In this uncomfortable dilemma the Government was eventually compelled to act. After thirteen Bills had been thrown out of Parliament, the School Boards for Elementary Education were set up in 1870, with the ingenious safeguard of the Cowper-Temple Clause added in 1891, which provided for religious instruction of a type that taught a just humility, an acceptance of the station in life to which God had called one, and the promise of extensive rewards in a heaven hereafter. (See page 124.)

It is clear, then, that the original purpose of the official educational system was to teach people just enough to be good and faithful servants, and to be able to read public notices telling them what they were not allowed to do.

It is equally clear that this system, which is so aptly called " elementary education," has greatly discouraged independent thought and that inquiring attitude of mind which has always been the mainspring of the full and creative life.

It is not surprising, therefore, that very few people have been sufficiently hardy to withstand the imposition of such a mental strait-jacket. Probably none has escaped undamaged in this respect.

Consequently, we are now faced with the desirability of creating social conditions in which all may have an equal opportunity to take part in every form of social activity. The situation in the world to-day provides us with the possibility of bringing this about. The Butler Education Bill, at the present moment before the House of Lords, will do much to assist in this, despite the rejection of a proposal to incorporate music in the general curriculum. Moreover, people must wake up to the fact that participation in music—whether creating it, performing it or listening to it—is essentially a social activity. The commercial aspect, which almost completely dominates any kind of music-making to-day, must be put in its proper place—on the shelf.

The delicacy of Bali music, the voluptuous romance of Arab songs, the fervour of French twelfth-century religious music, the scintillating brilliance of Mozart, the magnificence of Beethoven, the refined subtlety of Debussy, the transcendental flights of Schönberg, the vitality of Stravinsky, all evoke responses in me. There are, naturally, many aspects of this or

144

that art to which I am impervious. This or that composer simply does not strike on my box, if I may repeat an expression used earlier in this book. But the thing to aim at, to put it as if it were possible to employ a conscious act of volition in these matters, is enjoyment of as much as possible.

Enjoyment of music, that is the important thing. To take pleasure in listening to music. More: to take an active pleasure in listening. For it is not a passive business. The listener must always do his share, trying his best to comprehend, to co-operate with, the composer who, even although it is true to say that he writes music because he can't help it, must write with reference to an audience. And that audience is you.

**THE END**

# SUGGESTED GRAMOPHONE RECORDS

THE reader is referred to that excellent American publication, *The Gramophone Shop Encyclopedia of Recorded Music* (1936), for certain records marked with an *, as well as for many other recordings of early and unusual music which do not appear in English catalogues.

1. *Veni Sancte Spiritus,* Anon., Columbia History of Music, Record 5710.
2. *Mira Lege,* Anon., Col. Hist. Mus., Record 5710.
3. Sanctus from *Missa Papæ Marcelli,* Palestrina (florid Counterpoint), Col. Hist. Mus., Record 5712.
4. Sundanese Song *Udan mas* (Java), Parlophone " Music of the Orient," MO103.
5. *Gender Wajang,* " Selendero," Bali Music to a Shadow Play. Parlophone " Music of the Orient," MO105.
6. Modern Chinese Drama *Pang-tse,* " Nan-tien-men," Parlophone " Music of the Orient," MO103.
7. *Nachtzauber,* Wolf, Col. Hist. Mus., DB1234.
8. *Noël,* Fauré, LB42.
9. " Fantoches " from *Fêtes Galantes.* First Series, Debussy—unfortunately not obtainable singly—Album of the Songs of Debussy, DA1471–7.
10. Minuet from *Don Giovanni,* Mozart, DA977.
11. Allemande and Courante from Suite No. 8 in F minor for Harpsichord, Händel, Col. Hist. Mus., DB502.
12. Pavan and Galliard, *The Earl of Salisbury,* William Byrd, Col. Hist. Mus., Record 5712.
13. Passacaglia, Händel, DB1322. (This is not entirely satisfactory for my purpose. But see last movement of Brahms's Fourth Symphony, DB2253–7.)
14. *Sumer Is Icumen In,* Canon by John Fornsete (?), Col. Hist. Mus., Record 5715.
15. Fugue in E flat for Clavichord, Bach, L2242.
16. First Suite for Harpsichord, Purcell, Col. Hist. Mus., DB502.
17. Sonata for Harpsichord and Viola-da-Gamba, Bach, DB1322.
18. Sonata No. 1 in E flat, Haydn, DB1837.
19. Sonata in A major (K331), Mozart, DB1993.

20. Sonata in C minor (opus 111), Beethoven, LX491.
21. Symphony No. 41 in C major ("The Jupiter"), LX282.
22. *Orfeo*, Monteverde. (For this the Album of Selected Works by Monteverde is recommended, DB5038–42.)
23. *The Rite of Spring*, Stravinsky, D1919–22.
24. *L'Après-Midi d'un Faune*, Debussy (opening bars for solo flute), LX805.
25. *Daphnis and Chloe*, Ravel (opening bars for flute and clarinet arpeggii), D1826–7.
26. *The Planets*, "Neptune," Holst, L1542.
27. *Hänsel and Gretel*, Humperdinck, DB1758.
28. Clarinet Quintet, Mozart, LX624–7.
29. *Bolero*, Ravel, LX48–9.
30. *Till Eulenspiegel*, Strauss, E10925–6.*
31. *Violin Concerto*, Stravinsky, PD556173–5.*
32. *Symphony of Psalms*, Stravinsky, LX147–9.
33. *Don Giovanni*, Mozart, Vols. 7, 8, 9, The Mozart Society.
34. Second Symphony, Brahms, LX1515–9.
35. *Die Meistersinger, Overture*, Wagner, LX557.
36. *Don Quixote*, Strauss, LX186–90.
37. *Petrushka*, Stravinsky, DB3511–4.
38. *Symphonie Fantastique*, Berlioz, D2044–9.
39. *The Magic Flute* (Papageno's Music), Mozart, R979.
40. *Casse Noisette Suite*, Tchaikovsky, C2922–4.
41. *Carnaval Romain*, Berlioz (English Horn solo), LX570.
42. *L'Arlésienne*, Bizet, E10597–8.
43. *Das Rheingold*, Wagner (Anvils), D169, side 3.
44. The Madrigal (excellent examples of the English Madrigal are recorded in the Columbia History of Music):
    *Rest, Sweet Nymphs*, Pilkington; *Sing we and Chant It*, Morley, Record 5717.
    *As Vesta was from Latmos Hill Descending*, Weelkes; *The Silver Swan*, Gibbons; *Fair Phyllis*, Farmer, Record 5717.
45. *Fantasy for a Chest of Six Viols*, Weelkes, Col. Hist. Mus., Record 5714.
46. *Egmont*, Beethoven, DB1925.
47. *A Midsummer Night's Dream*, Mendelssohn, D1626–7.
48. *Hassan*, Delius, Vol. 3, The Delius Society.

49. *Third Piano Concerto,* Prokofiev, DB.1725–7.
       *Peter and the Wolf,* Prokofiev, DB3900–2.
50. Symphony No. 5, Shostakovich, DB3991–6.
51. Violin Concerto, Khachaturian, K1082–6.
52. *Song of the Fatherland,* Dunayevsky, FB2767.
       *Soviet Airmen's Song,* Dunayevsky, FB2767.
53. String Trio, Webern, K904.
54. *Lyric Suite for String Quartet,* Berg, CA8244–7.
55. Symphony, Hindemith, E164–9.
56. String Trio No. 2, Hindemith, LX311–3.
57. Duet for Viola and 'Cello, Hindemith, Col. Hist. Mus.,
       DB1789.
58. List of Recorded Works by Stravinsky:
       *The Song of the Nightingale,* D1932.
       *Petrushka,* DB3511–4.
       *The Rite of Spring,* LX119–23.
       *The Soldier's Tale,* LX197–9.
       *Les Noces,* LX326–8.
       Octet for Wind Instruments, LX308–9.
       Concertino for String Quartet (withdrawn).
       *Symphony of Psalms,* LX147–9.
       Capriccio for Piano and Orchestra, LX116–8.
       Violin Concerto, PD556173–5.
       Duo Concertant for Violin and Piano, CM199.
       *Apollon Musagètes,* X167–70.
       *Pulcinella,* LFX289, D15126.
       Serenade in A, C-LF139–40.
       *Firebird,* CM115.
       *Jeux de Cartes, Piano Rag-Music, Ragtime for* 11
       *Instruments,* LX382.
59. *The Enchanted Flute,* Ravel, DB1785.
60. String Quartet, Ravel, LY6105–7.
61. *Jeux d'Eau,* Ravel, DB1534.
62. Twelve Studies for Piano, Debussy, K891–6.
63. "En · fermant les yeux," from *Manon,* Massenet,
       DB3603. (This song should be compared with
       Mahler's *Ich atmet' einen linden Duft,* No.
       67 below.)
64. *Spanish Rhapsody,* Chabrier, E522.
65. Prelude, Chorale and Fugue, Franck, DB1299–1300.
66. Scherzo from String Quartet in E flat major, opus 109,
       Reger, G-EH886.*

67. *Ich atmet' einen linden Duft,* Mahler, Col. Hist. Mus., DB1787. (This song should be compared with Massenet's "En fermant les yeux," No. 63 above.)

68. *Das Buch der hängenden Gärten,* Schönberg, Col. Hist. Mus., DB1787.

69. *Ein Heldenleben,* Strauss, VM44.*

70. Overture to *Der Freischütz,* Weber, DB1874.

71. Overture to *Oberon,* Weber, DB3554.

72. Bridal Cortège from *Le Coq d'Or,* Rimsky-Korsakov, B8633.

73. *Le Poème d'Extase,* Scriabin, DB1706–7.

74. *Thamar,* Balakirev, DB4801–2.

75. Coronation Scene from *Boris Godunov,* Mussorgsky, DB900.

76. *Kaléidoscope,* Cui, DA1010.*

77. Polovtsi March from *Prince Igor,* Borodin, DB1683.

78. Overture to *Russlan and Ludmila,* Glinka, D1808.

79. Overture to *Zampa,* Hérold (old recording), C1818.

80. *Le Tambourin,* Rameau, E10514.

81. Couperin: available only in Couperin Society, one vol. of harpsichord music played by Landowska.

82. (a) Prelude to *Alceste,* (b) March from *Thésée,* (c) Notturno from *Le Triomphe de l'Amour,* Lully, DB1587.

83. Finale of Symphony No. 104 in D major, Haydn, LX856–8.

84. Finale of First Symphony in C major, Beethoven, DB3537–8.

85. Sinfonia in B flat major, J. C. Bach, D1988.

86. Dance of the Blessed Spirits from *Orpheus,* Gluck, D1784.

87. *La Bohème,* Puccini, DB3448–60.

88. "Non piangere, Lui," "Nessun dorma," from *Turandot,* Puccini, DA1075.

89. *Requiem,* Verdi, D1751–60.

90. *Aïda,* D1595, and *Rigoletto,* DX139, Verdi.

91. *Serenade to Music,* Vaughan Williams, LX757–8.
    *Overture to a Picaresque Comedy,* Arnold Bax, LX394.
    Symphony in G minor, E. J. Moeran, C3319–24.
    Concerto in E flat major, John Ireland, DX1072–4.

92. Concerto for Viola and Orchestra, William Walton, DB5953–5.

*Rio Grande,* Constant Lambert, L2373–4.
*Seven Sonnets of Michelangelo,* C3312, B9302.

93. " Blow, Blow, Thou Winter Wind," " Under the Green-wood Tree," from *As You Like It,* Arne, B4199.
94. *Dido and Æneas,* Purcell (Purcell Society).
95. *Rejoice in the Lord Alway,* Purcell, Col. Hist. Mus., DB500.
96. *Awake, Sweet Love,* Dowland, Col. Hist. Mus., Record 5715.
97. Harpsichord Concerto, Händel, DB3307–8.
98. " The Lord is a Man of War " from *Israel in Egypt,* Händel, LB20.
99. Fugue in F major for Organ, Buxtehude, G-FM23.*
100. Chorale-paraphrase: *Credo* for Organ, Scheidt, Anthologie Sonore.
101. *Banchetto musicale*: Suite No. 1 for Viols, Schein (American Society of Ancient Instruments), V-24792.*
102. *Also hat Gott die Welt geliebt,* five-part chorus, Schütz, K-38.*
103. Andante and Presto from Sonata in A major, Scarlatti, DB2847.
104. " May Sweet Oblivion Lull Thee," from *La Coronazione di Poppœa,* Monteverde, Col. Hist. Mus., DB500.
105. *Filiæ Jerusalem,* Gabrieli, G-D833.*
106. *Christe Redemptor* and *Conditor alme siderum,* Dufay, Col. Hist. Mus., Record 5711.
107. Conductus: *Beata viscera Mariae Virginis,* Pérotin; Organum Duplum: *Haec Dies,* Léonin, Lumen 3201.
108. Fourth Symphony, Tchaikovsky, DB2899–2903.

# INDEX

151

153

156

# LITERATURE

## THE SECOND COMMON READER
*Virginia Woolf  A 132*

The subjects range from the Elizabethans to D. H. Lawrence, including The Poems of Donne, Swift and Stella, De Quincey's Autobiography, Hazlitt, Defoe, Beau Brummell, Dr. Burney's Evening Party, Walter Scott, Aurora Leigh, Meredith, Hardy, Christina Rossetti, Edmund Gosse, and a number of other essays.

"I think," wrote Mrs. Woolf herself of this book, "one might describe it as an unprofessional book of criticism dealing with such lives and books as have chanced to come my way, rather from the point of view of a writer than of a student or critic. I have often no doubt been interested in a book as a novelist: but as often have read and written simply for amusement and without any wish to establish a theory."

## LIFE IN SHAKESPEARE'S ENGLAND
*J. Dover Wilson  A 143*

Extracts from writers contemporary with Shakespeare, arranged to illustrate the social atmosphere which surrounded the poet at different periods of his career, and is reflected in his work. The sections are England and the English: The Countryside: Superstition: Education: London: Books and Authors: The Theatre: The Court: House and Home: Rogues and Vagabonds: The Sea: An Elizabethan Day. An annotated glossary is appended.

## AN AUTOBIOGRAPHY
*R. G. Collingwood  A 136*

Professor Collingwood, Waynflete professor of Metaphysical Philosophy at Oxford, attained fame in two special fields: as a philosopher and as an expert on Roman Britain. But he was far more than a philosopher or an archaeologist or an historian: he was a humanist with a passionate belief in democratic ideals. This short account from his own hand of his life and how he shaped it, of his reaction to the influences of contemporary life and the modern climate of opinion, is a document of first importance for the understanding of the twentieth century.

# PELICAN BOOKS

# Lives of the Great Composers

A90, 91, 92

*EDITED BY A. L. BACHARACH*

Three Volumes

A book about composers, not about their compositions—"a ridiculous division of the indivisible," as the Editor admits. But the attempt has been made to show the man, explained if you will by his creative work, where that has been necessary and possible, rather than the work explained by the man.

The contents are:

## VOLUME ONE

## VOLUME TWO

## VOLUME THREE

# PELICAN BOOKS

# Ballet  Revised Edition                                    A 122

*ARNOLD HASKELL*

The first complete guide to Ballet for a few pence: its history, its theory, notes on the leading personalities and creators of modern ballet, studies in individual ballets and of some contemporary dancers, illustrated with photogravure plates and decorations by Kay Ambrose.

To the new edition an appendix has been added giving a brief history of Ballet in England during the War years.


# Opera                                                      S 40

*EDWARD J. DENT*

An introduction to Opera for those who are just beginning, or perhaps have not yet begun, to take an interest in it. It is an outline of the history of Opera from its beginnings, and the evolution of the operatic libretto, with special chapters on English Opera and Opera in England. Presented under various aspects—social, literary, dramatic and decorative. It is illustrated with sixteen pages of photogravure and decorations by Kay Ambrose.

" A genial, persuasive, plain-man's introduction to and story of opera as a social and literary, as well as a musical growth: a capital contribution to the badly needed new writing of musical history against the background of other arts, and of life. The author forges a strong lever to move our people opera-ward."—*Musical Times.*

---

# PELICAN BOOKS

# Recent and Forthcoming Penguins

# and Pelicans